Hannes Gumtau
Wolfgang Kurschatke

Englische Grammatik für den Realschulabschluss üben

MANZ VERLAG

Wolfgang Kurschatke, Realschullehrer.
Hannes Gumtau, Realschullehrer.
Sie sind erfolgreiche Autoren zahlreicher Lernhilfen.

3. Auflage 2004
Manz Verlag
© Ernst Klett Verlag GmbH, Stuttgart 2001
Alle Rechte vorbehalten
Lektorat: Harald Kotlarz, Rottenburg
Herstellung: Karin Schmid, Baldham
Umschlaggestaltung: Zembsch' Werkstatt, München
Titelbild: Premium, Faltner, Düsseldorf
Illustration: Sven Palmowski, Stuttgart
Layout: Karin Schmid, Baldham
Satz: Karin Schmid, Baldham
Druck: Druckhaus Beltz, Hemsbach
Printed in Germany

ISBN 3-7863-2025-X

Liebe Schülerin, lieber Schüler,

Wozu diese Lernhilfe?
Um englische Grammatik zu üben und sicher zu beherrschen, wenn es darauf ankommt.

Welche Grammatik?
Einfach alles, was immer wieder verlangt wird und wo sich erfahrungsgemäß Fehler einschleichen können.

Welches Ziel steckt dahinter?
Dich fit in englischer Grammatik zu machen, damit du in schriftlichen Arbeiten und in der Realschulabschlussprüfung keine Fehler machst (oder fast keine). Bestimmt hast du schon gemerkt, dass die Beherrschung der Grammatik für jede Art von Fragestellung in der Prüfung wichtig ist.

Wie solltest du vorgehen?

In drei Schritten zum Ziel:

1. Du wiederholst das Grundwissen.
In jeder Übung kannst du einen Aspekt einer grammatischen Form wiederholen.

Blickst du mal nicht durch, dann helfen dir die *tipps & tricks* weiter

2. Du wendest das Grundwissen an.
Im ersten Schritt hast du die Formen einzeln geübt, hier kommen sie alle zusammen vor, so wie auch in schriftlichen Arbeiten und beim Sprechen.

3. Du bearbeitest Prüfungsaufgaben.
Hier kannst du sehen, in welchen Aufgabentypen Grammatik vorkommt. Ob *guided writing* oder *vocabulary*, überall findest du „versteckte" Grammatikfragen.

Wenn du dieses Bild siehst, musst du Fehler selbst erkennen und korrigieren.

Lösungen zu allen Übungen findest du im hinteren Teil des Buches.

Alles klar? Dann kann's losgehen.

Viele Spaß und Erfolg dabei!

Inhalt

A Mengenbezeichnungen

Some und any

1. Look at the picture and then put in **some** or **any**.

a) Are there _____ lions on the farm? – No I can't see

   _____; but I can see _____ hens.

b) Are there _____ horses on the farm? – Yes, there are.

   There are _____ cows, too.

c) There's _____ tea in the pot, but we haven't got

   _____ sugar.

d) Have you _____ idea when the performance begins?

e) You can't have _____ more meat; we must save

   _____ for your brother.

f) Can I have _____ more tea, please? – Yes, of course.

2. **Say it in English.**

a) Frage Tom, ob er noch etwas Milch möchte.

_____?

b) Sage, dass du noch etwas Tee haben möchtest, aber ohne Zucker.

_____?

c) Sage, dass Tom auf der Farm Hühner, aber keine Gänse gesehen hat.

_____?

d) Frage Judy, ob sie in der Stadt Bücher oder CDs gekauft hat.

_____?

Du verwendest *some* vor allem in bejahten Aussagesätzen und *any* vor allem in verneinten Aussagesätzen und Fragen. *Some* steht auch in Fragen, die eine höfliche Bitte oder ein Angebot ausdrücken.

Zusammensetzungen mit *some* und *any*

3. **Something** or **anything**? **Someone** or **anyone**?
Somewhere or **anywhere**?

a) There was a noise outside. I heard _____ in the garden.

b) Did you see my hat _____? – No, I didn't see

it _____.

c) Shall we tell you _____ very interesting?

I don't want to hear _____. I am too tired.

d) Look. There's _____ in the car. It's a suitcase.

Can you see _____ in it? – No, I can't see

_____.

e) John is hungry. He wants _____ to eat, but

he doesn't want _____ to drink.

f)   Is there _____ in the fridge? I'm hungry. – I'm sorry,

there isn't _____ left. But I can go and get

_____ at the supermarket.

g)   Has _____ seen the dog? It must be

_____ in the garden.

h)   Susan didn't enjoy the party because she didn't know

_____.

i)   The doorbell is ringing. There must be _____ at the door.

much – many – a lot of

4.   Fill in **much**, **many** or **a lot of**.

a)   How _____ friends have you got? – I've got _____
friends.

b)   How _____ sugar do you take in your tea? – I don't take
_____ because I don't like it too sweet.

c)   How _____ animals are there on the farm? –
There aren't _____, they are on the hills.

d)   How _____ money did Tom spend? – He didn't spend
_____, he was nearly broke.

e)   How _____ times did you visit London? – I was there
_____ times last year.

f)   Tony got bad marks in his last test. There were _____ mistakes
in it.

Du nimmst *much* (= viel) bei nicht zählbaren Substantiven (z. B. *sugar*), *many* bei Substantiven im Plural (z. B. *animals*). Beide verwendest du meist in Fragen und verneinten Aussagesätzen. In bejahten Aussagesätzen nimmst du eher *a lot of* (= viele).

a little – a few

5. Fill in **a little** or **a few**.

a) There are only _____ potatoes left. We must go and buy some.

b) Robert is a good pupil. He only made _____ mistakes.

c) Diana only met _____ friends at the party. She was very disappointed.

d) The boys ate some sandwiches, but they only drank _____ of the alcohol.

e) There's _____ time left. We must hurry to catch the bus.

Bei nicht zählbaren Substantiven (z. B. *time*) nimmst du *a little* (= wenig), bei zählbaren (z. B. *potatoes*) nimmst du *a few* (= wenige).

each und every

6. Fill in **each** or **every**.

a) In the driving school there are tests _____ month.

b) _____ of the candidates had taken lessons before.

c) The lessons are £20 _____.

d) _____ time Lisa tried to start the car, it didn't go.

e) Fifty persons out of _____ hundred failed the test.

f) In _____ case the examiner had to take over the braking or steering.

g) _____ other day my friend practised driving.

Each heißt „jeder" von (aus einer bestimmten Anzahl), *every* bedeutet ganz allgemein „jeder".

9

7. Say it in English.

a) Sage, dass jeder in eurer Familie ein Auto hat.

_____

b) Sage, dass man überall Fahrschulen finden kann.

_____

c) Sage, dass es für einen Kandidaten unmöglich ist, alles zu wissen.

_____

d) Sage, dass heute jeder etwas über Autos wissen muss.

_____

Die **Zusammensetzungen** mit _every_ heißen: _**everyone**_ (= jeder), _**everything**_ (= alles) und _**everywhere**_ (= überall).

Vermischte Übungen

8. Fill in: **some – someone – something – somewhere – any – anyone – anything – anywhere – everyone – everything – everywhere.**

a) Is there _____ in the garden? – No, there isn't

_____ in the garden. But there is _____

in the house. I can hear _____ singing a song.

b) Are there _____ birds in the garden? – No, there aren't

because there are _____ cats on the lawn.

c) Is there _____ red on the house? – Yes, I can see

_____ I think it's a bird.

d) Let's go down to the lake. We'll find a nice place _____.

e) Which things are we going to take with us? We can't carry

_____.

f) We saw snack bars _____ we went in America.

9. Say it in English.

a) Frage Jean wie viel Milch noch da ist.

_____

b) Jean antwortet, dass noch viel Milch im Kühlschrank ist, aber nur ein wenig Apfelsaft.

_____

_____

c) Jean sagt, dass nur ein paar Zwiebeln da sind.

_____

d) Du fragst, wie viele du kaufen sollst.

_____

e) Jean sagt, dass du dich beeilen musst, weil nicht mehr viel Zeit bis zum Essen ist.

_____

Prüfungsaufgaben

10. Answer the questions in complete sentences.

a) How many hours a week does Michael work for in total? (twenty) (2)

_____

b) Why do some of the immigrant children have fewer language problems than others? (from India / English second language) (2)

_____

_____

11. Asking questions

You would like to know the price of the ticket. (2)

_____

12. Say it in English.

a)   Mr Best will wissen, wie viel das neue Fremdsprachenprogramm kostet: (2)

_____

b)   Er bedankt sich herzlich: (2)

_____

13. Translate into German.

a)   Life has not changed in America over the last few decades. (2)

_____

b)   They don't earn enough money to pay for someone. (2)

_____

c)   But this will only be possible if they beat countries like …,
some of whose players also play … (3)

_____ …

_____ …

d)   Each time the top event of the opening ceremony … (2)

_____ …

14. Underline the three mistakes and correct them. (3)

a)   Every of the boys wants to play in the team.   _____

b)   How many time have we left?   _____

c)   I can tell you something very interesting.   _____

d)   You must be very careful in each case.   _____

e)   The doorbell is ringing. There must be anyone outside.   _____

B Pronomen

Personalpronomen – Possessivpronomen – Reflexivpronomen – reziprokes Pronomen – Relativpronomen

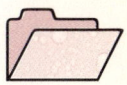

1. Fill in the missing pronouns.

a)   _I_____ open   __my____ eyes.   Can you see _me____?

b)   __You__ open   _____ eyes.   I can see   _____

c)   _____ opens   _____ eyes.   I can see   _____

d)   _____ opens   _____ eyes.   I can see   _____

e)   _____ opens   _____ eyes.   I can see   _____

f)   _____ open   _____ eyes.   Can you see _____?

g)   _____ open   _____ eyes.   We can see   _____

h)   _____ open   _____ eyes.   We can see   _____

Unterscheide die Personalpronomen in der **Subjektform** (z. B. *I, you, he, she, it, we, you, they*) und die in der **Objektform** (z. B. *me, you, him, her it, us, you, them*). Die **adjektivisch gebrauchten** Possessivpronomen sind: *my, your, his, her, its, our, your, their.*

2. **Replace the underlined words with pronouns.**

a)   <u>Tom</u> gives <u>Judy</u> a book.   _____ gives _____ a book.

b)   <u>Kathryn and Peter</u> invited   _____ invited _____ to
     <u>me and my brother</u> to their party.   their party.

c)   <u>Gemma</u> asked <u>the policeman</u>   _____ asked _____ the way.
     the way.

d)   Mr Brown invites <u>his boss</u>   _____ invites _____
     to his house.   to his house.

e)   <u>My brother and I</u> gave   _____ gave _____
     <u>the landlady</u> some flowers.   some flowers.

f)   <u>Tony</u> is selling <u>his car</u> next week.   _____ is selling _____
                                                next week.

3.   Fill in the correct possessive adjectives.

a)   Judy has got a new dress. _____ colour is white.

b)   Tom has got new inline skates. _____ hobby is skating.

c)   Mrs Dawson says: "Judy you must do _____ homework first."

d)   Mr and Mrs Dawson take _____ holidays in August.

e)   Mr Dawson says: "Let's take _____ bikes with us."

f)   Judy is taking _____ dog for a walk. _____ tail is wagging.

g)   Mr Dawson: "You must clean _____ bikes, children. They are dirty."

h)   Tom answers: "_____ bike isn't dirty. I cleaned it yesterday."

4.   Fill in the correct pronouns.

a)   This is Judy. _____ skirt is beautiful. _____ has fair hair.

b)   Judy has a friend. _____ name is John. _____ is a nice boy.

c)   _____ often go swimming at the weekends. _____ hobbies
     are swimming and dancing.

d)   _____ best friends are Gordon and Mary. Gordon says to John:
     "_____ hobby is tennis, but _____ like _____ hobbies,
     too, John."

5. Fill in the missing possessive pronouns.

a)   Give me the book.   It's _____.

b)   I give you the book.   It's _____.

c)   I give him the book.   It's _____.

d)   I give her the book.   It's _____.

e)   Give us the book.   It's _____.

f)   I give you the book.   It's _____.

g)   I give them the book.   It's _____.

6. Fill in the correct pronouns.

a)   Is this your father's car?   Yes, it's _____.

b)   This is not my book, Tony.   It must be _____.

c)   I've already invited all my friends. Has Judy invited _____?

d)   Is this your game, children?   No, it's not _____.

e)   This can't be your CD Jane.   I'm sure it's _____.

f)   I've already done my homework.   Have Tom and Judy done _____?

g)   This isn't Peter's bike.   _____ is old.

h)   This isn't my ball.   Is it _____,Tony?

                                            Yes, it's _____.

Die **substantivisch** gebrauchten **Possessivpronomen** *(mine, yours, his, hers, its, ours, yours, theirs)* stehen allein, nicht bei einem Substantiv wie die adjektivisch gebrauchten *(my, your, …)*.

7. Put in the suitable reflexive pronoun.

a)   We enjoyed _____ at the party last Saturday.

b)   The children hurt _____ badly when skating.

c)   The cat cut _____ on some broken glass.

d)   Jean, you must look after _____.

e)   Did you buy this new skirt, Judy? – No, I made it _____.

f)   Tom introduced _____ when he met Mrs Brown
for the first time.

g)   Judy blamed _____ for the mistakes she had made.

h)   Look into this mirror, Tom and Judy. You can see _____
there.

8. Translate.

a)   Judy fragt Tom, wo sie sich treffen können.

_____

b)   Tom antwortet, dass er sich nicht an das Café in der Nähe des Bahnhofs
erinnert.

_____

c)   Judy sagt, dass sich im letzten Jahr viel in der Stadt verändert hat.

_____

d)   Tom fragt, ob sie sich dem Jugendklub anschließen sollten.

_____

e)   Judy sagt, dass sich dort nicht viel ereignet.

_____

f)   Tom fragt sich, ob sie dort viele Freunde treffen werden.

_____

Das **Reflexivpronomen** *(myself, yourself, himself, herself, itself, ourselves, yourselves, themselves)* wird rückbezüglich gebraucht oder es dient zur Hervorhebung eines Substantivs.
Beachte die Unterschiede: *to meet* = **sich** treffen

9.   **Fill in the correct reflexive or reciprocal pronoun where necessary.**

a)   Sabine and Tom looked at _____ in the mirror, before

they went to the party.

b)   Sabine and Tom looked at _____ surprised when they

happened to meet.

c)   Sabine has changed _____ very much recently.

d)   Sabine and Tom get along with _____ very well.

e)   Sabine will always remember _____ her stay in England.

f)   Sabine's friend is very practical. He repairs his car _____.

Das reziproke Pronomen *(each other)* verwendest du, wenn du eine wechselseitige Beziehung (sich gegenseitig, einander) ausdrückst.

10.   **Say it in English.**

Sage deinem Freund, dass
a)   ihr euch lange nicht mehr gesehen habt.

_____

b)   du ihm nicht helfen kannst und dass er seine Hausaufgaben selbst
machen muss.

_____

_____

c)   du dich entschuldigst, wenn du zu spät kommst.

_____

d)   ihr euch auf der Party sehr amüsiert habt.

_____

e)   Tom und Mary sich im Kino getroffen haben.

_____

11. Fill in: **who** or **which**.

a)   I have a friend _____ speaks excellent Japanese.

b)   The letter _____ arrived yesterday is from my aunt in Canada.

c)   The film is about animals _____ live in the jungle.

d)   The boys _____ painted the graffiti on the wall had to remove it.

e)   The book is about a lady _____ spent ten years in Africa.

f)   Where can I find a shop _____ sells T-shirts?

g)   Sheila only eats food _____ is grown in her own garden.

Du verwendest *who* für **Personen**, *which* für **Sachen** (und Tiere).
Beide sind hier Subjekt eines Relativsatzes, z.B. *the girl who works* –
das Mädchen, das arbeitet (Wer arbeitet?)

12. Fill in: **who** or **whose**.

a)   Katie is the girl _____ won first prize.

b)   James is the boy _____ parents have just moved here.

c)   Debbie is the girl _____ mother works in the school canteen.

d)   Where is the house _____ windows were broken?

e)   Mrs Potter is the lady _____ passed her driving test yesterday.

f)   Is this the girl _____ bike was stolen?

g)   Where is the shop _____ owner is your cousin?

Du bezeichnest mit **whose** eine **Zugehörigkeit** oder einen **Besitz**, z. B. *the shop whose owner* – der Laden, dessen Besitzer. Dagegen ist *who* hier Subjekt im Relativsatz, z. B. *the man who* – der Mann, der.

13. Fill in **who** or **which** if necessary.

a)   The friends _____ I have invited haven't come yet.

b)   The window _____ they broke has now been repaired.

c)   David found the purse _____ his sister had lost.

d)   The car _____ stopped in front of our house is a BMW.

e)   The film _____ we wanted to see was no longer showing.

f)   Paul is the boy _____ has invited us to his birthday party.

g)   The music _____ Rebecca likes best is by the Beatles.

h)   Emma was the only girl _____ spoke a little French.

i)   Could you return the money _____ I lent you last week?

Die Relativpronomen *who* bzw. *which* können **Subjekt** bzw. **Objekt** sein. Wenn sie als **Objekt** verwendet werden, fallen sie fast immer weg, also: *The money which I lent you.* ▶ *The money I lent you.* Vorsicht beim Übersetzen ins Deutsche! Hier erscheint das Relativpronomen wieder: Das Geld, **das** ich dir geliehen habe.

14. Put the preposition at the end of the relative clause and drop the relative pronoun.

a) John visited the town in which he was brought up.

_____

b) The girl to whom you spoke is from form 9C.

_____

c) This is the bus on which we came.

_____

d) The country to which you are pointing is Ireland.

_____

e) Is this the book in which you are interested?

_____

f) The tourists to whom Emma was talking were from India.

_____

g) India is a country about which I don't know very much.

_____

h) The keys for which you are looking are on the shelf.

_____

Die **Präposition** steht fast immer am **Ende** des Relativsatzes, also:
The man to whom I spoke is Mr Potter. ▶ *The man I spoke to is Mr Potter.*

15. Join the two sentences.

a) Simon lives in New York. He is Emma's penfriend.

_____

b) Jennifer will be 16 next week. Her sister is in my class.

_____

c) Darren joined our club. You met him yesterday.

_____

d) These bikes are new. They belong to my friends.

_____

Diese Relativsätze enthalten zusätzliche Informationen, die nicht unbe-
dingt notwendig sind. Man nennt sie „nicht bestimmende Relativsätze"
(non-defining relative clauses). Sie werden immer durch **Kommas** vom
Hauptsatz getrennt. Man darf das Relativpronomen nicht weglassen und
man darf nicht *that* anstelle von *who* bzw. *which* verwenden.

Vermischte Übungen

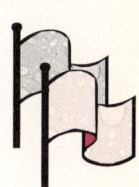

16. Fill in the correct pronouns if necessary.

a) After a month in England, Sabine joined _____ a group
of young people.

b) At the first meeting she introduced _____ to all the boys
and girls.

c) The group meets _____ every Friday night.

d) They enjoy _____ playing games and dancing.

e) Sabine wondered _____ how she could have stayed
a month with her first family.

f) She couldn't remember _____ having met such nice people
before.

g) They had a barbecue and Sabine and two other girls did all the
preparations _____.

h) When one of the girls was cutting the meat, she hurt
_____ with a sharp knife.

i)   When the guests came, they helped _____ to the food and drinks.

17. Say it in English.

a)   Die Gäste fühlten sich sehr hungrig.

_____

b)   Herr Brown mischte sich selbst einen Cocktail.

_____

c)   Er konnte sich nicht erinnern, so viele nette Leute getroffen zu haben.

_____

d)   Sein Freund und er haben sich viele Jahre nicht gesehen.

_____

e)   Als es läutete, ging Herr Brown selbst zur Tür und öffnete.

_____

18. Complete the sentences.

a)   Simon, _____ (?) father is an electrician, is my neighbour.

b)   An electrician is a man _____ (?) installs electric cables.

c)   He often repairs TV sets and cassette recorders _____ (?) don't work.

d)   A hammer is a tool with _____ (?) you can drive nails into wood.

e)   The children saw some birds _____ (?) feathers were blue and red.

19. Combine the following sentences.

a)   The boy must stay in hospital. He broke his arm yesterday.

_____

b)   The young man wanted to speak to my sister. He rang up last night.

_____

c)   A car hit a cat. It was running across the road.

_____

d)   There were five men in the pub. They were dirty and dangerous.

_____

e)   They were waiting with Jake. His friend was a beggar.

_____

f)   The men saw two police cars. They stopped outside.

_____

g)   The police interviewed a man. They thought they had stolen a car.

_____

20. Translate into English.

a)   Das Buch, das ich gelesen habe, ist sehr spannend.

_____

b)   Die Geschichte, die Simon erzählt hat, ist nicht wahr.

_____

c)   Das Mädchen, mit dem Simon tanzte, kommt aus Frankreich.

_____

d)   Emma, deren Schwester gerade in Schottland ist, ist meine Freundin.

_____

e)   Der junge Mann, der bei dem Unfall verletzt wurde, ist im Krankenhaus.

_____

21. Define the following words. Use relative clauses.

a) A manager _____

b) Immigrants _____

c) A housewife _____

d) A dinosaur _____

e) A burglar _____

f) A skyscraper _____

g) A pioneer _____

h) A computer freak _____

Prüfungsaufgaben

22. Complete the following text. Use the correct form of the words in brackets and find words of your own to replace the question marks.

a) Those _____ (?) are skilled in older programming languages _____ (?) are more likely to create problems in the new millennium have an advantage. (2)

b) Steven Spielberg made his own silent film "Amblin", in _____ (?) two hitchhikers were trying to get to California. (1)

c) The boy runs a group _____ (?) is called "Free the Children". (1)

d) He filled out his ticket order _____ (?) amounted to $1,200. (1)

23. Language: Join the two sentences with a suitable relative clause.

a)   The athletes arrived in their home town. They had competed in the Games. (2)

_____

b)   Rachel was dancing around happily. Her team had won a medal. (2)

_____

c)   The winner was interviewed after the competition. The competition had been really exciting. (2)

_____

_____

24. Define the following words in complete sentences.

a)   A guard (3)   _____

b)   A debt (3)   _____

c)   An expert (3)   _____

d)   Confetti (3)   _____

e)   A teenager (3)   _____

f)   Commercials (3)   _____

25. Translate into German.

a)   The factory employs 13.000 people, who wear cheap plastic shoes, because none of them can afford the shoes they make. (4)

_____

_____

b)   "To you in Europe the shoes we make have an image of freedom," she says. (3)

_____

_____

c)   Fans will feel the enthusiasm that has made this sport the fastest-growing. (3)

_____

d)   Anna, whom teachers describe as extremely bright, is perhaps an exception. (3)

_____

_____

e)   Her former English teacher says that there are children who have to stay on much longer. (3)

_____

_____

26. Underline the four mistakes and correct them. (4)

a)   Mr Smith's car, who is standing outside, can do 120 miles an hour.

_____

b)   That's the bus for it I've been waiting for three hours.

_____

c)   Mr Parson, who is our English teacher, is a nice person.

_____

d)   Mr Parson, who I was speaking, has always got time for us.

_____

e)   The church you are looking at is a wonderful building.

_____

f)   Susy Brown we met at the party who is my girlfriend.

_____

C Adjektiv – Adverb

Steigerung des Adjektivs

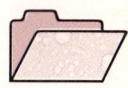

1. Fill in the adjectives in their correct forms or find other suitable words.

Four girls of the Abingdon Youth Club are preparing for a swimming competition.

a) Debby Pope is _____ (tall) of the girls and she is an _____ (excellent) swimmer. Debby is _____ (old) than most other girls.

b) Rebecca Jackson is only ten years old and she is _____ (young) of them. Of course, it is _____ (difficult) for her to win than for the other girls because they are _____ (strong) than her.

c) Lucy Parker is _____ (pretty) girl, and she is wearing a _____ (expensive) bathing costume than the others. Lucy has won _____ (many) races this month than Rebecca, but at the moment she is not _____ good _____ last year.

d) Angela Miller is _____ (ambitious) than her friends. Unfortunately, she had hurt herself last winter, and so she had _____ (little) training than before and she took part in _____ (few) competitions than she had expected.

e) For Patricia Baker _____ (important) thing is to meet nice people. Her trainer says: "You could be much _____ (good) if you tried harder."

Steigerung mit **-er / -est** *(big – bigger – the biggest)*, mit **more / most** *(difficult – more difficult – the most difficult)* oder unregelmäßig *(good – better – the best)*. Vergleich mit *(not)* **as ... as** – (nicht) so ... wie; mit **than** – als, z. B. *bigger than / more interesting than* – größer / interessanter als; höchste Steigerungsstufe: *the biggest / the most difficult* – der / die / das größte / schwierigste bzw. am größten / schwierigsten.

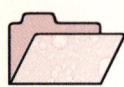

Bildung und Anwendung des Adverbs

2. Form the adverb.

a)   Kate smiled _____ (happy) when she saw Peter.

b)   Jason sat in his room _____ (quiet).

c)   The girls spoke _____ (friendly).

d)   Sarah can speak French _____ (fluent).

e)   Mark understands German _____ (good).

f)   Julie listened _____ (careful) to her teacher.

g)   Margaret came down from the tree _____ (safe).

h)   Paul could answer all questions _____ (quick).

Du bildest das **Adverb** normalerweise so: **Adjektiv + -ly = Adverb.** Es gibt auch **Sonderformen**, wie *good – well, lovely – in a lovely way, fast – fast*. Beachte die Rechtschreibung, z. B. bei *safe – safely, easy – easily, automatic – automatically*!

3. Adjective and adverb. Fill in the correct form of the words.

a)   easy   English grammar is not always _____. But you can

_____ do this exercise. It's an _____ one.

b)   angry   Our teacher was _____ today. He was shouting

_____ because we were so loud.

c)   **good**   Patricia can speak French _____. Her Spanish is

_____, too.

d)   **usual**   What's your _____ breakfast? – We _____

have cornflakes with milk and toast with jam.

e)   **slow**   The bus was _____. It went _____ up

the hill.

4. Translate into English.

Peter has come back from a language school in England.
Er berichtet:

a)   Ich kann Englisch jetzt gut verstehen.
b)   Meine Grammatik ist noch nicht perfekt.
c)   Aber ich kann fließend sprechen.
d)   Ich muss noch lernen, schwierige Wörter richtig zu schreiben.

a)   _____

b)   _____

c)   _____

d)   _____

_____

5. Answer the questions.

a)   How was school? – It was _____ (real, boring)

b)   How were your teachers? – They were _____

(terrible, strict)

c)   How was your English test? – It was _____

(extreme, difficult)

d)   How did you come home? – Oh, that't a good question. Paul's father

drove us home. He is an _____ (awful, good)

driver and he drove _____ (real, quick)

> Das **Adjektiv** bestimmt ein Substantiv oder Pronomen näher, z. B. *Peter is good, he is good.* Das **Adverb** beschreibt ein Verb, z. B. *Peter understands well*, ein Adjektiv, z. B. *(He is) really good* oder ein anderes Adverb, z. B. *(He drives) really quickly.* Beachte die **Schreibung**: *true – truly, extreme – extremely, terrible – terribly*!

6.   Choose the right word. Fill in: **fair – fairly, hard – hardly, high – highly, near – nearly, late – lately.**

a)   Simon jumped very _____ in the athletics

competition, and his result was _____ appreciated.

b)   Jonathan lives _____ the bus stop, but he

_____ missed his bus this morning.

c)   Jenny had to work _____ for her exam and she could

_____ believe that she would pass it.

d)   Claire got up _____ this morning and was _____

for school. This has happened several times _____.

e)   Andy saw a _____ match. All the players were

_____ good and nobody was hurt.

> Achte auf die verschiedene Bedeutung der sich ähnlich sehenden Adverbien, z. B. *hard* – hart, schwer; *hardly* – kaum.

Steigerung des Adverbs

7.   Fill in the comparative forms.

a)   Jane works carefully, but her sister works even _____

than she does.

b) Bill runs very fast. He can run _____ than his friends.

c) Jessica plays squash well. She can play it _____ than her little sister.

d) Jane's little brother eats very quickly. He eats _____ than the rest of the family.

e) Bill worked hard. In fact he worked _____ than the other boys.

f) We arrived early. We arrived even _____ than we had expected.

g) Tim takes sport seriously. He takes it _____ than other boys in his class.

8. Form the superlative.

a) Paul ran fast. He ran _____ _____ of all competitors.

b) Susan likes swimming very much. She likes it _____ _____ of all.

c) Jack went very far. He went _____ _____ of all climbers.

d) Jenny sings beautifully. She sings _____ _____ of all.

e) Harry answered sensibly. He answered _____ _____ of all.

f) Keith plays tennis well. He plays _____ _____ of all his team.

Adverbien auf -ly werden mit **more** bzw. **most** gesteigert, z. B. *quickly – more quickly – most quickly*. Beachte **Sonderformen**, wie *well – better – best, badly – worse – worst*!

Adjektiv nach Zustandsverben

9. Complete.

a) Susan looks very _____ (happy) today.

b) Her friend Sharon doesn't feel _____ (sad) either.

c) The flowers in the vase smell _____ (wonderful)

d) The birthday cake tastes _____ (delicious)

e) The music sounds _____ (good), but it is a bit

_____ (loud)

f) The little children were playing _____ (happy) in the

swimming pool.

g) When the lights went out they all felt their way

_____ (careful) in the dark.

h) Janet looks _____ (nice) in her new dress.

Nach manchen Verben folgt das **Adjektiv** (nicht das Adverb!) – wenn sie einen **Zustand** oder eine **Eigenschaft** beschreiben. Unterscheide: *She looks happy.* – Sie sieht glücklich aus (= Sie ist glücklich). *She looks happily at him.* – Sie schaut ihn glücklich an.

Vermischte Übungen

10. Guided Writing.

Peter has invited his Scottish friend Ian to visit him next summer. Here he gives information on his home town. What does he write?

Peter berichtet ihm, dass …
a) München größer als Edinburgh ist;
b) es die größte Stadt in Bayern ist;
c) dort eines der bedeutendsten Museen Deutschlands ist;
d) vielleicht ein völlig neues Fußballstadion gebaut wird.

a) *Munich is* _____

b) _____

c) _____

d) _____

11. Translate into German.

Steven visited an Indian reservation in the U.S.A. and wrote some information to his penpal Hans.

a) I didn't have the slightest idea how the native Americans live before I visited the reservation.

_____

_____

b) The Navajos are one of the most famous Indian tribes.

_____

c) More and more of them want to live in reservations.

_____

d) It's awful to hear that Indians have the highest alcoholic rate in the country.

_____

_____

e) They have a lower standard of education than white Americans and poorer health conditions.

_____

_____

12. Adjective or adverb? Write down the correct forms.

a) The Taylors like eating in pubs _____ (regular)

b) They think a pub is a _____ (popular) place where you can meet local people and enjoy the _____

_____ (extreme, warm) atmosphere there.

c) In their favourite pub "The Globe Inn" the food looks _____ (good) and it _____ (real) tastes _____ (excellent)

13.

Complete the text. Fill in adjectives or adverbs.

Alan and Sheila are good friends.

a)   Alan is good at most sports; he is even _____ (good)

than his elder brother and he often runs _____ (quick)

of all his class.

b)   The two are good at school, because they work _____

(quick) and _____ (accurate) than other pupils.

c)   Sheila's brother is the _____ (bad) and _____ (lazy)

boy in the school, but she knows that he is _____ (clever)

than he shows.

d)   David spends _____ (much) of his time at the tennis court

where he is one of the _____ (good) players around. He is able

to play very _____ (hard) and _____ (effective)

Prüfungsaufgaben

14.

Paraphrase the expressions in bold print.

a)   Twenty young people were **seriously injured** in an accident. (2)
They were _____

b)   Some boys, **especially** those who were standing had slight cuts. (1)
Some boys, _____ *those who were standing,*

had slight cuts. _____

c)   The ambulance arrived **at once**. (1)
It arrived _____

15. Use words of the same families as the ones in brackets.

a) The captain of the Titanic was _____ (confidence) enough to believe that his ship was unsinkable. (1)

b) The _____ (tragedy) accident happened 88 years ago. (1)

c) It was caused by a combination of poor planning and _____ (fool) decisions. (1)

d) The ship was designed to be the _____ (safety) with its 16 watertight compartments. (1)

e) The passengers did not know how _____ (danger) icebergs are. (1)

16. Adjective or adverb? Write down the correct forms.

a) Sydney is the _____ city of Australia (important). (1)

b) It is _____ away from Europe than Perth (far). (1)

c) Ayers Rock is Australia's _____ tourist attraction (popular). (1)

d) For most of Australia the _____ month is January (hot). (1)

17. Complete the following text. Use the correct form of the words in brackets and find a word of your own to replace the question mark.

The song "Tie a Yellow Ribbon ..." became a national symbol for Americans during the period form November 1979 to January 1981. They were waiting for 52 men and women to come home after they had been held prisoner in Iran for more a) _____ (?) (1) a year. This was one of the b) _____ (bad) periods in the US-Iranian relationship. But the positive aspect was that a c) _____ (real,

remarkable) (2) spirit of d) _____ (nation) (1) unity
developed. People sent lots of letters to local newspapers and
e) _____ (many) (1) Americans than ever used a yellow ribbon
to show their f) _____ (deep) (1) love and care for people in
need.

18. Writing a letter.

In a letter to his English pen-friend Sebastian tried to describe a dinosaur.
Look at the picture and the German prompts and continue his letter.

Dear Chris,
Last week I watched "Jurassic Park" and I liked it very much. In a book
I found some interesting information about these strange creatures.
My favourite one was the brontosaurus.

▶   (ein riesiges Tier)
▶   (mindestens sechs Meter hoch
          und dreißig Meter lang)
▶   (dicke Beine wie ein Elefant)
▶   (und winziger Kopf)

The brontosaurus was a ._____ (1)

It was _____ (3)

It had _____ (2)

and a _____. (1)

19. Translate into German.

a)   When Spielberg first thougt of making his most important film
      "Schindler's List", he was not sure if he could do it. (3)

      _____

      _____

b)   Believing that other colleagues were better qualified for such a serious
      subject, he tried to sell the rights to more experienced directors. (4)

      _____

      _____

c)   However, none of them was really interested. (2)

_____

d)   Many of his friends told him he would definitely fail. (2)

_____

e)   But the more doubts they expressed, the more certain Spielberg became. (2)

_____

20. **Underline the four mistakes and correct them.** (4)

a)   Susan thinks she is beautifuller than her friends.

_____

b)   She can cook very good.

_____

c)   Her pizza tastes well.

_____

d)   She can work very quickly.

_____

e)   She is quicker as most other girls.

_____

f)   Her friend David is the nicest boy around.

_____

D Zeitformen

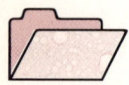

Simple present

1. **What they do at the weekend.**

a) Simon _____ (play) football every afternoon.

b) Darren often _____ (go) for long walks in the park.

c) Patrick _____ (sit) most of the weekend in front of the TV.

d) Sheila and John _____ (not watch) TV at all.

e) They sometimes _____ (visit) their grandma on Saturday.

f) They _____ (not stay) there the whole afternoon.

2. **Say it in English.**

You talk to an American friend about your daily routine.

a) Ich stehe gewöhnlich um 7 Uhr auf.

_____

b) Mein Schulbus geht um 20 vor 8.

_____

c) Die erste Stunde beginnt immer um 8 Uhr.

_____

d) Am Nachmittag gehe ich zum Fußballtraining.

_____

e) Nach dem Abendessen sitze ich etwas vor dem Fernseher.

_____

f)   Am Samstag stehe ich nicht so früh auf, weil wir nicht in die Schule gehen.

_____

_____

Mit dem *simple present* berichtest du über etwas, das regelmäßig, oft oder gewohnheitsmäßig geschieht. Achte auf die Endung: *he comes, she goes, he cries*!

Present progressive

3.   **What are they doing?**

a)   Where is John? – He _____ (tidy) his room.

He can't go out yet because it _____ (rain) very hard.

b)   Look, Darren _____ (lie) on the sofa.

He _____ (read) a book.

c)   Martin and his father _____ (work) in the garage.

They _____ (repair) the bikes.

d)   What can you hear? – Rachel _____ (play)

the guitar. Ann and Sheila _____ (listen) to her.

e)   What _____ (you do)?

– I _____ (repeat) the tenses.

4.   **Say it in English.**

Rebecca is just talking to her German friend Kathi. She wants to know what they are doing.

a)   Ich backe gerade einen Kuchen.

_____

b)   Mutter feiert ihren Geburtstag.

_____

c)   Susan ist beim Einkaufen.

_____

d)   Sie kauft Kaffee und Blumen.

_____

e)   Nur Paul macht nichts. – Oh doch, er spielt Tischtennis.

_____

Mit dem *present progressive* drückst du aus, was gerade geschieht. Vorsicht bei der Schreibung: *come* ♦ *coming, cut* ♦ *cutting;* *tidy* ♦ *tidying*!

Simple past

5.   What happened yesterday?

a)   Yesterday Rebecca _____ (decide) to go to a disco.

b)   She _____ (not walk); she _____ (go) by bus.

c)   There _____ (not be) many people at the disco; it _____ (be) early.

d)   Rebecca _____ (meet) a girlfriend and they _____ (sit) down.

e)   The disc jockey _____ (tell) some jokes but she _____ _____ (not understand) everything; the music _____ (be) too loud.

f)   When a boy from her class _____ (enter) the room, they _____ (dance) together. They _____ (stay) there until 11 o'clock.

6. **Say it in English.**

Peter is back from England. He is reporting about his stay in London.

a)   Letzte Woche waren wir in London.

_____

b)   Wir besuchten den „Rock Circus" und den „Dungeon of London".

_____

c)   Wir trafen nette Leute und gingen dann in ein Pub.

_____

d)   Wir aßen einige Sandwiches, aber wir bekamen kein Bier.

_____

e)   Der Wirt wollte unsere Ausweise sehen.

_____

f)   Dann sagte er: „Ihr seid zu jung für Alkohol."

_____

Mit dem _simple past_ berichtest du über Vorgänge, die in der Vergangenheit stattfanden. Achte auf **Signalwörter** wie _yesterday, last week, last year_ und andere.

Past progressive

7.   **What were Simon's friends doing yesterday in the afternoon?**

a)   Yesterday afternoon Paul _____ (play) tennis.

b)   His two sisters _____ (swim) in the pool.

c)   Jenny _____ (read) a detective story.

d)   Lucy _____ (knit) a pullover for her little sister.

e)   Angela _____ (repair) her bike.

f)   Jane and George _____ (prepare) for a maths test.

8.   Fill in: simple past or past progressive.

a)   It _____ (rain) this morning when the girls

_____ (go) to the bus stop.

b)   Darren _____ (write) a letter yesterday when

his mother _____ (come) into his room and

_____ (ask) him to help her.

c)   When the school bell _____ (ring), all the pupils

_____ (pack) their schoolbags and

_____ (run) to the door.

d)   Lucy _____ (read) a comic under her desk when

her teacher _____ (come) and _____

(look) at her.

e)   Patrick _____ (mend) his bike this afternoon

when the telephone _____ (ring).

Mit dem *past progressive* drückst du aus, was zu einer bestimmten Zeit in der Vergangenheit gerade passierte, z. B. *He was playing tennis.* – Er hat (gerade) Tennis gespielt. Du kannst auch über eine stattfindende Handlung berichten, z. B. *he was mending* – er hat gerade repariert, die durch eine andere, die im *simple past* steht, z. B. *the telephone rang* – das Telefon läutete, unterbrochen wurde.

Present perfect

9.   Complete the sentences using the present perfect.

a)   Where is Debbie? – I _____ (not see) her

since last week.

b)   Bill likes Susan. – He _____ (know) her for two months.

c)   The bike is all right. – I _____ (repair) it.

d)   Lucy's room is in a mess. – She _____ (not tidy) it yet.

e) The Hubers know England well. – They _____ (be) there
ten times.

f) Steven is hungry. – He _____ (not eat) anything
since 8 o'clock.

10. Translate into English.

a) Julie ist traurig; sie hat ihre Schlüssel verloren.

_____

b) Wir müssen warten; der Zug ist noch nicht angekommen.

_____

c) Ist Patrick da? – Er ist gerade nach Hause gekommen.

_____

d) Ich habe mein Zimmer aufgeräumt; jetzt kann ich spielen gehen.

_____

_____

e) Ich habe mein Fahrrad schon seit vier Jahren; es fährt immer noch gut.

_____

_____

f) Jenny war noch nie in London. Wie schade!

_____

Mit dem *present perfect* berichtest du über etwas, das sich auf die Gegen-
wart auswirkt; was bisher oft geschehen ist bzw. noch nicht abgeschlossen
ist oder sich zu einer unbestimmten Zeit in der Vergangenheit abgespielt
hat. **Signale** sind z. B. *since 1999* – seit 1999; *for two days (now)* – (jetzt)
seit zwei Tagen; *often* – schon oft; *never* – noch nie; *not yet* – bisher noch
nicht.

Present perfect progressive

11. Use the present perfect progressive to complete the sentences.

a) I must stop now. I _____ (work) for five hours.

b) Tom is angry. He _____ (wait) for Andrea for over an hour.

c) The weather is awful. It _____ (rain) all day.

d) This is my parents' house. They _____ (live) here since 1999.

e) Jack is exhausted. He _____ (paint) the house all morning.

f) I _____ (try) to phone Martin, but the line was engaged.

g) Jackie likes music; she _____ (play) the piano for ten years.

12. Say it in English.

a) Wie lange lernst du schon Englisch? – Ich lerne es schon seit 5 Jahren.

_____

_____

b) Dieses Buch ist nicht neu. Wie lange benutzt du es schon? – Wir benutzen es schon seit Anfang des Schuljahres.

_____

_____

c) Dein kleiner Bruder ist so schmutzig. – Er hat den ganzen Morgen Fußball gespielt.

_____

_____

d)   Dein Vater ist sehr müde. – Er hat den ganzen Tag im Garten gearbeitet.

_____

_____

Mit dem *present perfect progressive* berichtest du über etwas, das in der Vergangenheit begonnen hat und noch andauert (*since 8 o'clock* – seit 8 Uhr, *for two hours now* – jetzt schon seit zwei Stunden) oder schon lange andauert (z. B. *all morning* – schon den ganzen Morgen). Im Deutschen nimmst du oft das Präsens mit „schon"!

Past perfect

13. Answer the questions. Use the simple past and past perfect in your answers.

a)   When did you go to bed last night? – (watch the film on TV)

I _____ to bed after I _____

the film on TV.

b)   When did Sheila drive to the youth club? – (finish her homework)

Sheila _____ to the youth club after she _____

her homework.

c)   Why did Jane buy a new dress? – (want to go to a party)

Jane _____ a new dress because she _____

to go to a party. But unfortunately she fell ill.

d)   When did Kenneth phone his friend? – (go into town)

Kenneth _____ his friend after he _____

into town.

e)   When did the pupils begin to chatter? – (teacher leave the classroom)

The pupils _____ to chatter after the teacher _____

the classroom.

f)   Why did Emma not come in time? – (miss the bus)

Emma _____ in time last night because she

_____ the bus.

Mit dem **past perfect** berichtest du über weit zurückliegende Vorgänge. Das weiter zurückliegende Geschehen steht im **past perfect**, das näher liegende im **simple past**. Beachte mögliche Signale: *after* – nachdem, *when* – als, *before* – ehe, *because* – weil. Das **past perfect** verwendest du auch im if-Satz Typ 3: *I would have told you the answer if I had known it.*

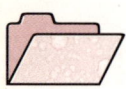

Will-future

14. Make sentences using the elements given and add the will-future.

a)   I'm sure / we / enjoy / our winter holidays

_____

b)   I hope / there be / enough snow

_____

c)   It / not be / easy to find / cheap accommodation

_____

·d)   We / have to book / the rooms / next week

_____

e)   I / be / fifteen / in January

_____

f)   I think / we / have / a wonderful party / in the snow

_____

15. Say it in English.

Translate the weather forecast for an English guest.

a)   Morgen früh wird es in den Bergen bewölkt sein,
b)   aber am Nachmittag wird die Sonne scheinen.
c)   Übermorgen wird es wärmer sein, aber etwas windig.

d) Das Wetter wird sich in den nächsten Tagen wenig ändern.
e) Es wird sicher nicht regnen.

a) _____

b) _____

c) _____

d) _____

e) _____

Du nimmst **will-future** für zukünftige Geschehen, die du nicht beein-
flussen kannst. Hinweise sind z. B. *I think* – ich denke, *I hope* – ich hoffe,
I'm sure – ich bin sicher, *I expect* – ich erwarte. Halte auseinander:
*I **won't*** = *I will not* – ich werde nicht – *I want* – ich will!

Going to-future

16. What are they (not) going to do next week?

a) Mr Miller / paint his house

_____

b) His wife / buy new curtains

_____

c) The children / attend a language course

_____

d) They / not watch TV / next Saturday

_____

e) They / have / a big party / on Saturday night

_____

f) They / have / lots of food and drinks

_____

47

17. Say it in English.

Sage was deine Freunde vorhaben.

a)   Paul: Ich will Martin treffen; wir haben vor, ein paar CDs zu kaufen.
b)   Helen: Ich habe vor, mit meiner Mutter einkaufen zu gehen.
             Ich brauche einen Mantel.
c)   Barbara: Meine Schwester und ich werden Karten für das Musical kaufen.
             Wir wollen die Vorstellung am Samstag besuchen.

a)   Paul wants to meet Martin. They _____

     _____

b)   Helen _____

     _____

c)   Barbara _____

     _____

Mit dem *going to-future* drückst du eine feste Absicht, einen Plan oder
ein Vorhaben aus.

Vermischte Übungen

18. Write down the correct forms of the verbs given in brackets.

a)   Patrick Miller, sixteen years old, has a girlfriend. He and Jennifer

     _____ (meet) ten months ago at their local youth

     centre, and they _____ (go) out ever since.

b)   Patrick _____ (have) plenty of jobs already.

c)   But now he _____ (work) in a

     supermarket, filling the shelves and sweeping the floor.

d)   He only _____ (spend) some of the money

     on dances and drinks.

e)   The rest _____ (save)

f)   It _____ (help) to pay for his college education

after leaving High School.

19. Fill in the correct tense.

Debbie is interviewing Patrick, a new pupil at Macclesfield High School.

Debbie: When _____ you _____ (arrive)

in Macclesfield?

Patrick: My family _____ (come) here last Saturday.

At first everything _____ (be) so new and exciting

for me.

Debbie: Where _____ (be) you from?

Patrick: Well, we _____ (live) in a small town

in Kent for ten years, but my father _____ (lose)

his job six months ago and, fortunately, he _____

(find) a new one in Manchester.

Debbie: How _____ you _____ (like) Macclesfield?

Patrick. Well, I _____ (not see) much of the town yet.

I _____ (spend) most of the time unpacking

boxes.

Debbie: _____ you _____ (like) our school?

Patrick. Yes, I _____. The classmates _____ (be) very nice

and Simon Moore often _____ (help) me with

the homework. We _____ (use) other textbooks

in Kent.

Debbie: What sports _____ you _____

(practise)?

Patrick: Well, I _____ (be) good at hockey. I _____

(play) it for five years now. I think I _____ (join)

the local club soon.

Debbie: _____ (have) a good time here. Thank you.

Patrick: _____ (?).

20. Guided Writing.

a)   David begrüßt Steven und fragt nach seinen Plänen für die Sommerferien.

_____

_____?

b)   Steven sagt, dass er letztes Jahr in Kanada war und dass ihm die Reise
sehr viel Spaß bereitet hat. Er möchte wieder nach Kanada.

_____

_____

_____

c)   David sagt, dass er bisher noch nicht in Kanada gewesen ist. Er hoffe aber,
in zwei Jahren seine Tante in Toronto besuchen zu können.

_____

_____

_____

Achte auf die **Signale**:
last year – letztes Jahr ▶ *simple past*,
not ... yet – (bisher) noch nicht ▶ *present perfect*,
in two years – in zwei Jahren ▶ *future*

Prüfungsaufgaben

21. Fill in the correct forms of the verbs given in brackets. (4)

a)   The city of Sydney _____ (hold) the Olympic Games
       in 2000.

b)   The Olympic Games of 1992 _____ (take place) in
       Barcelona.

c)   Since 1896 a lot of athletes from all over the world _____
       (compete) in Olympic Games.

d)   Usually millions of people _____ (watch) the events on TV.

22. **Complete the following text. Use the correct form of the words
       in brackets.**

Sheila Wright a)_____ (live) (1) in Cheltenham. She
b) _____ (just, come) (2) back from a school
trip to London. She c) _____ (wear) (1) a new pair of
shoes. Looking at them her mother says, "Why d) _____
(you, buy) (1) these shoes in London?" Sheila replies that they are
"Doc Martens", and they e) _____ (invent) (1) in the
forties by Claus Maertens who f) _____ (experiment) (1)
with old tyres to make a pair of shoes after g) _____
(injure) (1) his foot. He h) _____ (succeed, get)
(2) a patent on the heavy shoe with the thick sole. Since the eighties
the "DMs" i) _____ (become) (1) a fashion item.

23. The Iceberg Comes

When Edith Brown Hausman last saw her daddy 88 years ago he was standing on the deck of the Titanic, smoking a cigar and smiling at his wife and daughter. "I'll see you in New York", he said confidently, as his family was taken to Lifeboat No. 14. Edith and her mother watched as the band played a hymn, the lights went out and in a terrible roar everything on the supership seemed to break loose. And then it was gone, along with Mr Brown and over 1,522 other souls. …

Even today, the Titanic tragedy lives on in the human imagination and in books, films, plays and even on the Internet. One of the reasons is that it is a story of superlatives. …

Answer in complete sentences.

a)   When did Edith see her father last? (1/1)

_____

b)   What was he doing then? (1/1)

_____

c)   Where did he hope to see his wife and daughter again? (1/1)

_____

d)   Why do people talk about the tragedy even today? (1/1)

_____

24. Personal question. Write complete sentences.

What are your personal hopes or fears for the future? You may use these words: **job, partner, family – enjoy, find, get on well with.** (2/2)

_____

_____

_____

_____

25. Guided Writing.

You want to invite your American friend Joey to come with you on the luxury liner "Hanseatic". You are now writing a fax to him talking about the notes you have made on the German brochure. (10)

c) *eigene Filme mitbringen?*

a) *jeden Abend Discomusik*

MS HANSEATIC

AUSSTATTUNG	KABINEN	LEISTUNGEN
7 Decks	88 Außenkabinen (22	Kreuzfahrt mit allen
Band, Disco,	qm) mit 176 Betten 4	Bordleistungen
Unterhaltungsprogramm	Suiten (44qm)	Eine mit Softdrinks
Frühstücks- und	Minibar/TV/Video	gefüllte Minibar in der
Mittagsbuffett	Klimaanlage	Kabine für die Dauer
Vortragsraum/Kino	Satellitentelefon	der Reise
Fitneßraum/Sauna	Kabinen 401 424 mit	eigene Reiseleitung
Swimmingpool und	Bullaugen, alle anderen	mit organisierten
Poolbar	Kabinen mit großen	Ausflügen
Massage/Whirlpool	Fenstern	Reiseunterlagen mit
Bibliothek, Videothek		länderkundlichen
Eigenes Bordfernsehen		Informationen

b) *viele Sport-möglichkeiten*

Dear Joey,

I a) _____ (write) you this letter because I

b) _____ (win) a trip for two people on the "Hanseatic"

and I c) _____ (like) to invite you to come

with me. There d) _____ (be) a disco every evening and there

e) _____ (be) lots of sports facilities. There f) _____ (be)

a video recorder in our room and we g) _____ (take) our

own films with us. I hope you h) _____ (come) with

me. I i) _____ (look forward) j) _____

(see) you on the "Hanseatic".

Best wishes, Dominik.

26. Translate into German.

a)   After four years of involuntary absence, Vingo S. was welcomed home
spectacularly by his wife and three kids. (4)

_____

_____

b)   It was a happy ending to a story that had taken a tragic turn four years before, when Vingo was imprisoned. (3)

_____

_____

c)   What was the crime he had committed? (1)

_____

d)   He worked in his uncle's bank, and when his uncle suddenly disappeared, he was accused of being a criminal. (4)

_____

_____

27. Underline the five mistakes and correct them. (5)

a)   Jennifer has visited Rome last summer.

_____

b)   Darren has been away since Monday.

_____

c)   Keith is a member of our youth club for two years now.

_____

d)   Helen is going to buy a new shirt tomorrow.

_____

e)   Angela gave the video back after she has seen it.

_____

f)   When Sheila entered the room, Patrick slept.

_____

g)   Barbara listens to the radio just now.

_____

E *Fragesätze*

Entscheidungsfragen

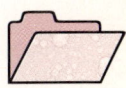

1.   Questions about school.

a)   _____?

  – Yes, school begins at eight o'clock

b)   _____?

  – Yes, there are lessons every afternoon.

c)   _____?

  – Yes, we have lunch at school.

d)   _____?

  – No, we don't go to school on Saturday.

e)   _____?

  – No, I haven't visited our twin town in Germany yet.

2.   Guided Writing: Asking questions.

  Julia is a new pupil in your class. You want to know whether she …
a)   is interested in sports
b)   likes tennis
c)   saw the match last night
d)   wants to play a game against you
e)   can meet you at ten o'clock tomorrow.

a)   _____

b)   _____

c)   _____

d)   _____

e)   _____

Entscheidungsfragen haben kein Fragewort. Die Antwort lautet *yes* oder *no*. Du nimmst ein vorhandenes **Hilfsverb** (z. B. *be, can*) oder das Ersatzhilfsverb *do / does* bzw. *did*.

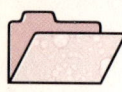

Fragen mit einem Fragewort

3. Ask for the information which you can't see.

a) The first lesson begins at ??? every morning.

_____?

b) The pupils can buy refreshments in the ???.

_____?

c) Andy went to the club last week because ???.

_____?

d) Most pupils work very ???.

_____?

e) Homework takes ??? hours a day.

_____?

f) The school uniform costs ??? £.

_____?

g) Jennifer came to school by ???.

_____?

h) Darren must get up at ??? every morning.

_____?

Diese Fragen beginnen mit einem **Fragewort**: *when* – wann?; *where* – wo?; *how* – wie?, *how much* – wie viel?; *how many* – wie viele?; *why* – warum? Nach dem Fragewort folgt ein Hilfsverb (z. B. *can*) oder das Ersatzhilfsverb *do / does / did*.

4. Ask for the object of the sentences.

a) Simon wrote a letter.

_____?

b) Fred likes hockey.

_____?

c) Jane bought a camera.

_____?

d) Julia and Emma will visit their aunt.

_____?

e) They have read a French newspaper.

_____?

f) Oliver helps his mother in the afternoon.

_____?

g) Darren lost his camera.

_____?

Mit *who* (auch: *whom*) – wen? bzw. *what* – was? fragst du nach dem **Objekt** des Satzes. Nach dem Fragewort folgt ein Hilfsverb (z. B. *have, will, can*) oder das Ersatzhilfsverb *do / does / did*.

5. Ask for the information that you can't see.

a) ??? loves Julia.

_____?

b) ??? went to Italy in her summer holidays.

_____?

c) The ??? happened in front of the school.

_____?

d)   The **???** begins at nine o'clock.

_____?

e)   **???**'s friend plays the guitar.

_____?

f)   Bus **???** goes to the railway station.

_____?

g)   **???** children came to the birthday party.

_____?

Mit *who* – wer?; *which* – welcher?; *which of you* – wer von euch?; *what* – was?; *whose* – wessen? fragst du nach dem **Subjekt** des Satzes. Es gibt keine Umschreibung mit *do / does / did*!

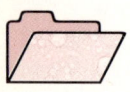

Verneinte Fragen

6.   **Make up negative questions.**

a)   Who plays cricket?

_____?

b)   Which of you knows the answer?

_____?

c)   Why did Jack stay in Dublin?

_____?

d)   When can Sheila go home?

_____?

e)   Which books belong to you?

_____?

f)   How many of you like rugby?

_____?

g)   Who came to the barbecue?

_____?

Bei **verneinten Fragen – auch bei verneinten Subjektfragen** – gilt das Gleiche wie bei verneinten Aussagen: Du brauchst in jedem Fall ein Hilfsverb (z. B. *can*) oder ein Ersatzhilfsverb *do / does / did*. Also: *Who comes?* ◆ *Who doesn't come? What happened?* ◆ *What didn't happen?*

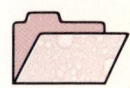

Fragen mit nachgestellter Präposition

7.   Ask for the words in bold print.

a)   Geoff comes from **Manchester**.

_____?

b)   He is good at **music and sport**.

_____?

c)   He goes to **a large comprehensive** school.

_____?

d)   The old Rover belongs to **his father**.

_____?

e)   He bought it from **an old lady**.

_____?

f)   He sometimes listens to **classical music**.

_____?

g)   Geoff and his friends are talking about **their summer holidays**.

_____?

h)   They are afraid of **too much rain**.

_____?

Du beginnst mit dem Fragewort und stellst **die Präposition ans Ende**. Beachte den Unterschied zum Deutschen:

*Who is it **from**?* *What are you talking **about**?*
Von wem ist es? **Über** was redet ihr? ,

Angehängte Kurzfragen *(question tags)*

8.   Add a question tag.

a)   Julia is sixteen now, _____?

b)   She has got three brothers, _____?

c)   She can speak German, _____?

d)   Jason isn't very tall, _____?

e)   They cycle to school, _____?

f)   Julia doesn't play the violin, _____?

g)   Martin went to London last week, _____?

h)   He'll come to Germany next summer, _____?

Auf eine **positive Aussage** folgt eine **negative Kurzfrage** (z. B. *She is* ▶ *isn't she?*). Auf eine **negative Aussage** folgt eine **positive Kurzfrage** (z. B. *He isn't* ▶ *is he?*). Du nimmst ein Hilfsverb bzw. *do / does / did* anstelle eines Vollverbs.

Vermischte Übungen

9.   An interview with a boy from Scotland.

Ian is staying in your town for a while. Ask him some questions using the elements given:

a)   What time / get up / every morning?

_____

b) How / get to school?

_____

c) Like / school?

_____

d) What / do / in your spare time?

_____

e) Which / favourite soccer team?

_____

f) know / a German football club?

_____

g) Where / learn / German?

_____

h) Which places / see / so far?

_____

10. An American girl is visiting your class. Ask her some questions.

Du möchtest gern wissen, …

a) wo sie herkommt;

_____

b) ob sie Geschwister hat;

_____

c) wie ihr Deutschland gefällt;

_____

d) was ihr an einer deutschen Schule nicht gefällt;

_____

e) ob sie schon früher in Europa war;

_____

f)   was ihre Hobbys sind;

_____

g)   wie lange sie bleiben wird;

_____

h)   ob sie einen Freund hat.

_____

11. An interview for a job.

Mrs Collins is asking Katie a few personal questions. What does she say?

Mrs Collins wants to know …

a)   whether Katie knows any foreign languages;

_____

b)   what schools she went to;

_____

c)   which her favourite subjects at school were;

_____

d)   which subjects she didn't like at all;

_____

e)   where she usually spends her weekends;

_____

f)   why she would like to become a secretary;

_____

g)   how she is going to come to the office every day;

_____

h)   when she will be able to start work.

_____

12. You have decided to visit London. Your pen-friend advised you to buy a special Travelcard because it is the most economical way to travel in London. But you need some more information.

You would like to know …

a)   the price for the ticket;

_____?

b)   where to buy it;

_____?

c)   when to use it;

_____?

d)   whether your friend has ever used the Travelcard herself.

_____?

Prüfungsaufgaben

13. A famous athlete opens a new Fitness Centre in his home town. You get the chance to talk to him. Write down your questions. (4)

You want to know …

a)   when he won his first medal;

_____

b)   whether he knows any sportsmen who take drugs;

_____

c)   why he decided to become an athlete;

_____

d)   how long he practises every day.

_____

14. You are driving along Route 66. You talk to the attendant at a gas station and you ask him about … (4)

a)   motels;

_____

b)   number of visitors at the Route 66 festival last month;

_____

c)   any serious accidents nearby;

_____

d)   TV series ROUTE 66.

_____

15. Guided Writing.

Michael, a German computer freak, is walking around a computer fair in Munich. He is talking to Mr Best, the representative of an American firm.

a)   Mr Best (fragt, ob er ihm behilflich sein könnte): (2)

_____?

b)   Michael (erkundigt sich nach Sonderangeboten): (2)

_____?

c)   Michael (will wissen, wie viel das neue Fremdsprachenprogramm kostet): (2)

_____?

d)   Michael (möchte herausfinden, ob Mr Best es empfehlen könne): (2)

_____?

e)   Michael (fragt, welche Übungen Kunden in den USA bevorzugen): (2)

_____?

16. Defective dialogue.
Ask the questions.

The Oxford College Magazine interviewed students on their job activities.
Write down the questions. The answers are here: (6)

a) _____?

Because I don't get enough money from my parents to buy clothes I like.

b) _____?

Of course, there are. In my store we always call the police. Shoplifters are
a nuisance.

c) _____?

My job – it's mostly exciting and well-paid.

17. Underline the mistakes and correct them. (5)

Ask your colleague:

a) Who do you live?

_____

b) How many brothers and sisters do you have?

_____

c) What do you at the weekend?

_____

d) Can you speak French?

_____

e) Which sport like you?

_____

F Modalverben

Fähigkeit: *can – could – be able to*

1. Fill in: **can – can't – couldn't – be able to.**
Foreign languages

a) Catherine has a penfriend in Hamburg. She _____ speak a little
German, but she _____ speak French.

b) She wants to go to a language school and hopes that she
_____ speak French, too.

c) When her brother was ten, he _____ speak German;
he started to learn it when he was twelve.

d) Their parents _____ only speak English because they have
never learnt another language. So they _____ speak German
or French.

e) When they were in Paris last summer they _____ understand
what people were saying to each other.

2. Say it in English.

a) Ich kann dir leider nicht helfen.

_____

b) Gestern konnte ich nicht Tennis spielen, weil es geregnet hat.

_____

c) Ich habe Tom noch nicht anrufen können; ich kann seine Telefonnummer
nicht finden.

_____

d) Nächsten Samstag werde ich nicht zum Training kommen können.

_____

e)   Ich könnte dir helfen, wenn du mich vorher anrufst.

    _____

Für **„können"** kannst du im *present* can oder *am / is / are able to*
nehmen. **Die anderen Zeiten** bildest du mit der entsprechenden Form
von *be able to.* **Could** heißt meist „könnte"; *could not* bedeutet –
je nach Zusammenhang – „konnte nicht" oder „könnte nicht".

Erlaubnis – Verbot: *can – can't – mustn't*

3.   Fill in: **can – may – can't – mustn't – be allowed to.**

a)   _____ we play in the garden? – Yes, of course.

    But you _____ be too loud; grandmother wants to have a rest.

b)   Don't drive so fast! You _____ drive faster than twenty miles

    an hour near the the school.

c)   You _____ sit here, but you _____ smoke in this room.

d)   Excuse me, _____ I take the magazine? – Oh yes, you

    _____ keep it.

e)   Yesterday there was a big birthday party. The children _____

    stay up late.

f)   Next summer Helen _____ go on holiday

    without her parents.

g)   We came to the beach two days ago, but we _____

    _____ (go) swimming yet because the sea is very rough.

4.   Translate.

    Susan schreibt ihrer Brieffreundin in Schottland:

a)   Während der Woche darf ich abends nicht ausgehen.

    _____

b)   Am Wochenende darf ich bis 10 Uhr wegbleiben.

_____

c)   Letzten Freitag durfte ich ins Konzert gehen.

_____

d)   Nächstes Jahr werde ich mit meinen Freundinnen nach Italien fahren dürfen.

_____

Für **„dürfen"** kannst du im _present_ can oder _am / is / are allowed to_ nehmen. Für die anderen Zeiten brauchst du die entsprechende Form von _be allowed to_. Ein **Verbot** drückst du mit _can't_ aus, ein ausdrückliches Verbot mit _mustn't_ – nicht dürfen. Mit _may_ – dürfen, fragst du sehr höflich, ob du darfst.

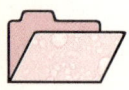

Notwendigkeit, Zwang: _must – need not – have to_

5.   Complete.

a)   Today is Friday. Mrs Fleming has been ill since Monday. Her husband and the children _____ do a lot of work in the house.

b)   Yesterday Darren _____ cook dinner.

– _____ he _____ do the washing too? –

No, he _____.

c)   On Wednesday Pamela _____ water the flowers in the garden, but she _____ cut the lawn.

d)   Mr Fleming _____ go shopping all the week.

e)   Mrs Fleming _____ go to her doctor next Monday to have a check up and get some medicine if necessary.

6. Say it in English.

a) Wir müssen diesen Monat viel lernen.

_____

b) Gestern mussten wir einen langen Aufsatz schreiben.

_____

c) Morgen werden wir eine schwierige Matheaufgabe machen müssen.

_____

d) Wir haben seit zwei Wochen ein Projekt vorbereiten müssen.

_____

e) Am Freitag müssen wir nicht zur Schule kommen.

_____

Für „müssen" kannst du im **present** *must* oder *has to / have to* nehmen;
„nicht müssen" heißt *need not* oder *doesn't have to / don't have to*.
Für die anderen Zeiten nimmst du die entsprechende Form von *have to*.

Möglichkeit, Wahrscheinlichkeit: *may – might*

7. Use **may – might – may have – might have**.

a) Bill isn't at home. He _____ be in the fitness centre.
He's quite often there.

b) Jane isn't on the bus. She _____ gone by bike.
It isn't raining.

c) Kate _____ lend you her racket, but I don't think she will.

d) Tom _____ helped you if you had asked him.

e) You _____ be right, but I don't think they will believe you.

f) Darren's team lost the match. They _____ won if
they hadn't been so ineffective.

May bedeutet „kann" bzw. „vielleicht", z. B. *it may rain soon* – vielleicht regnet es bald; es kann bald regnen. Mit *might* – könnte vielleicht, drückst du eine recht unsichere Vermutung aus. Beachte die Frage: *May I sit here?* – Darf ich hier sitzen?

Ratschlag, Verpflichtung: *should – ought to*

8.   Use **should – shouldn't – should have – shouldn't have**.

a)   The music is very loud. You _____ turn the loudspeaker down.

b)   Cigarettes are not good for your health. You _____ smoke so much.

c)   Your room is in a mess. You _____ tidy it.

d)   You're late. You _____ taken an earlier bus.

e)   Your keys are gone. You _____ left them on the fence.

f)   Your essay isn't good. You _____ tried harder.

Should heißt „sollte". Für *should* kannst du *ought to* nehmen. Mit *should* + *past participle* bzw. *ought to* + *past participle* drückst du aus, dass etwas hätte sein sollen.

Vermischte Übungen

9.   Fill in: **can – mustn't – needn't**.

a)   You _____ stay at home, Darren. You _____ come with me. I _____ do the shopping by myself.

b)   We're early. We _____ run so fast; we _____ walk slowly.

c)   It isn't cold outside. So we _____ put on our coats. We _____ wear our jackets.

d)   It's a very important meeting. You _____ forget to come.

e)   _____ we park here? Yes, of course, but you _____
       forget to be back before eight o'clock when we close the gate.

f)   Jennifer _____ be back home by 10 o'clock. She
       _____ be late because her dad will be angry.

10. Can you give advice?

a)   Peter can't swim. ▶ He ._____ jump into deep water.

b)   Paul has missed his school bus. ▶ He _____ got up earlier.

c)   There are no lessons on Saturday. ▶ You _____ get up early.

d)   Sussex Road is very busy. ▶ Pedestrians _____ cross it;
       they _____ use the subway.

e)   When you go to an interview for a job you _____ wear
       a T-shirt and jeans. ▶ You _____ put on
       a jacket and trousers.

f)   You see this traffic sign:

       ▶ You _____
       drive very carefully,
       and you _____ drive too fast.

11. Translate into German.

a)   May we sit here? – Oh, yes.

       _____

b)   It may rain tomorrow. Shall we change our plans?

       _____

c)   Could you show me the bus stop, please?

_____

d)   Jennifer could not come to our party because she was ill last week.

_____

e)   You mustn't leave the door open, Barbara. It's windy.

_____

f)   You needn't help me, Darren. I can do it myself.

_____

12. Translate into German: modal verb + have been.

a)   I can't find my key. I must have forgotten it.

_____

b)   It's a pity you dropped the vase. You should have been more careful.

_____

c)   You needn't have come so early. The meeting starts in half an hour.

_____

d)   I waved at Peter in the street but he didn't react; he may have been
     in a hurry.

_____

e)   The accident was awful. It might have been even worse if the ambulance
     hadn't come quickly.

_____

f)   Sheila can't have forgotten the date, she is so reliable.

_____

Du willst sagen, dass etwas hätte sein sollen – *should have been* / *ought
to have*; ..., sein müssen – *must have* ...; vielleicht sein sollen – *may have ...
/ might have* ... bzw. sein können – *can have* ... *(been).*

Prüfungsaufgaben

13. Personal questions.

a) What can you do to protect the environment? Name two different aspects and explain. (lights? electricity?) (2/2)

_____

_____

b) Give a brief description of what life might be like in the year 3000? (transport? health?) (2/2)

_____

_____

c) What do you have to do when there is a fire alarm at your school? (2/2)

_____

_____

14. It is important for every Californian to know how to reduce dangers. Look at the signs and write down what you must do or should avoid before, during and after an earthquake, and say why.

Before:

a) You _____ have a First Aid Kit so that you _____ help injured people. (3)

During:

b) You _____ smoke or light a match because the flames _____ cause an explosion. (3)

After:

c) You _____ listen to the news to get information about what to do next. (3)

15. Translate into German.

This is a letter which an American housewife wrote to her mother
to complain about her husband:

a)   Dear Mum, you may remember that Jack decided to buy a computer
three months ago. (3)

_____

_____

b)   Since then there has been a radical change in his attitude to his family. (2)

_____

_____

c)   Every day he spends hours and hours on his computer trying out
new programs. (2)

_____

_____

d)   Even on the weekends Jack cannot resist sitting in front of the monitor. (2)

_____

_____

e)   I think it might be a good idea to ask Uncle Herbert for advice. (2)

_____

f)   He should be able to tell me what to do. (2)

_____

16. Underline four mistakes in the German translation and correct them. (5)

a)   You mustn't take this bus.   Du musst diesen Bus nicht nehmen.

_____

b)   It may snow tomorrow.   Es darf morgen schneien.

_____

c)   Can we stay here?   Dürfen wir hier bleiben?

_____

d)   Could you help me, please?   Konntest du mir bitte helfen?

_____

e)   He should come earlier.   Er soll früher kommen.

_____

G Passiv

Simple present – present progressive

1. Say what happens or is happening.

a)   The lawn _____ (cut) at the moment.

b)   All the playing fields _____ (cut) every week.

c)   Cars _____ (repair) at a garage.

d)   I can't visit you because my car _____ (repair)

e)   You mustn't enter the room. A candidate _____ (test)

f)   The candidates _____ (not, test) at the same time.

Simple past – past progressive

2. Say what happened or was happening.

a)   John couldn't go swimming last week because the swimming pool
_____ (clean)

b)   The room is not dirty. It _____ (clean) yesterday.

c)   The bridge _____ (build) when we wanted
to cross the river.

d)   A lot of bridges _____ (build) in the past.

e)   In the little cafe snacks _____ (serve) all the day.

f)   When we came in some of the customers _____
(serve)

Du bildest das **Passiv** mit einer Form von *to be* und dem *past participle* (Partizip Perfekt / 3. Form des Verbs). Du kannst auch **modale Hilfsverben** und *be* und das *past participle* verwenden. Die *progressive form* (= Verlaufsform) bildest du im *present* mit *am / are / is* + *being* + *past participle* und im *past* mit *was / were* + *being* + *past participle*.

Present perfect

3. Say what has happened.

a) Ten thousand pounds _____ (steal) from the bank.

b) This letter _____ (write) perfectly.

c) I hope only correct answers _____ (give)

d) All their problems _____ (solve)

e) A lot of work _____ (do) today.

f) Smoking in schools _____ (not, allow) for some years.

g) My friend lost his bike. It _____ (not, find) yet.

h) Angela _____ (never, invite) to a party.

Will-future

4.   **Say what will happen.**

a)   My car _____ (not, repair)

until next week.

b)   The final match _____ (show) on TV.

c)   Difficult questions _____ (ask) by the examiner.

d)   A lot of windows _____ (smash)

by the hooligans.

e)   A new supermarket _____ (open)

next month.

f)   All my friends _____ (invite)

to my party.

g)   The building _____ (not, complete)

until next year.

h)   Angela's film _____ (develop)

by Friday.

Modalverben

5.   **Say what can, must, should, ought to, has to be done.**

a)   Your car is dirty. It _____ (should wash).

b)   The door _____ (cannot, shut).

The lock is broken.

c)   Sheila's room _____ (ought to, tidy).

It's in a mess.

d) There were a lot of clouds. The mountains _____
_____ (could not, see)

e) Grandma is ill. She _____
(must, look after)

f) Susan _____ (might, invite)
to John's party.

g) The old house is a ruin. It _____
(have to, pull down) next year.

h) Chinese is a difficult language. It _____
(cannot, learn) easily.

i) Tony _____ (not, ought to, laugh at)
by the other boys.

j) This kind of work _____ (can, only, do)
with the help of computers.

k) The house _____ (must, sell)
by the end of summer.

l) The washing-up _____ (have to, do)
by the boys.

m) The private office _____ (must, not,
enter).

n) The fire _____ (could, not, put out)
because there wasn't enough water.

Vermischte Übungen

6.   Make sentences in the passive. Find the right tense.

a)   English _____ (understand) all over the world.

b)   Angela _____ (invite) to our party next week.

c)   A thriller _____ (show) on TV last night.

d)   A lot of money _____ (earn) in professional football.

e)   The match _____ (win) by our team next Sunday.

f)   The Brown's house _____ (build) twenty years ago.

g)   The new building _____ (not, finish) yet.

h)   Our new school _____ (finish) by next summer.

i)   This problem _____ (must, discuss)
     by our headmaster tomorrow.

j)   German _____ (not, teach) in all English schools.

k)   Bavarian beer _____ (always, be) famous.

l)   Great progress _____ (make) in computer
     technology in recent years.

m)   I can't tell you the time. My watch _____ (repair).

n)   We couldn't cross the river because a new bridge _____
     (build). The old one was dangerous.

Achte auf Signalwörter (z. B. *next Sunday, not yet, last night*) und bilde
dann die richtige Zeitform.

7. Active or passive?

a) The first Olympic Games of modern times _____ (to take place) in Paris.

b) In ancient Greece the Games _____ (to celebrate) in the form of religious festivals.

c) The earliest Olympic Games _____ (to take place) about 776 BC.

d) There _____ (to be) originally four towns where the Games _____ (to hold)

e) The events _____ (to include) all sorts of competitions, like running, throwing, wrestling.

f) The winners _____ (to treat) like modern professionals.

g) Baron de Coubertin _____ (to renew) the old tradition.

h) Since then the Olympic Games _____ (to hold) again every four years with only two exceptions during the two World Wars.

i) When a city _____ (to apply) for the Games, a lot of sports facilities _____ (must, to build)

j) Since 1896 more and more athletes _____ (to invite) to take part in the competitions.

k) Today all big sports events _____ (to show) on television.

Beachte Signalwörter (z. B. Zeitangaben oder *since*) und achte auf den Sinnzusammenhang, bevor du dich für die richtige Zeitform und für Aktiv oder Passiv entscheidest.

8.   Translate into German.

a)   Mrs Carter was offered a better job.

_____

b)   Last night the doctor was sent for.

_____

c)   The team will be offered a great chance.

_____

d)   Mr Johnson is supposed to fly to Paris next week.

_____

e)   It was said that Mr Brown would find another job.

_____

Manche Passivsätze kannst du mit „man" im Deutschen wiedergeben.

9.   Say it in English.

a)   Sage, dass man eine Fähre nach England sehr früh buchen muss.

_____

b)   Sage, dass man dir einen Brief schrieb.

_____

c)   Sage, dass man dir ein gutes Hotel angeboten hat.

_____

d)   Sage, dass man dir bald ein gutes Angebot schicken wird.

_____

e)   Sage, dass man deinen Freund ebenfalls eingeladen hat.

_____

Beachte, dass gewöhnlich das **indirekte Objekt** (z. B. *I, my friend*) zum **Subjekt** im Passivsatz wird.

Prüfungsaufgaben

10. Put in the correct forms of the words in brackets or find a word of your own.

a) Even as a child Carl Sagan _____ (fascinate) by the night sky. (2)

b) When Sagan was 12 years old he _____ (???) by his grandfather what he wanted to be. (2)

c) Although many of the watertight compartments _____ (damage), most passengers had no idea … (2)

d) She _____ (interview) by a reporter from London. (2)

e) The following sentences _____ (take) from a novel. (2)

f) She really liked the voice that _____ (chose) for the computer. (2)

11. Translate into German.

a) You are more likely to be believed later. (3)

_____

b) I have made a film that has been called the most expensive one. (4)

_____

_____

c) Most stunt people were seriously injured. (3)

_____

d) Since then the Olympic Games have been held again. (3)

_____

e) Eni is paid 25 cents an hour. (2)

_____

f)   They are often forced to work until midnight. (2)

_____

g)   Two fingers were cut off. (2)

_____

12. Underline the five mistakes and correct them. (5)

a)   Shorts and T-shirts is worn in summer.

_____

b)   The fish is being frying in a pan.

_____

c)   The new potatoes will be planted in spring.

_____

d)   Buses are drove by bus-drivers.

_____

e)   Cold drinks must keeping in a fridge.

_____

f)   Tony sagt, er sei ein guter Spieler. (= Tony is said to be a good player.)

_____

H Gerund – Infinitiv

Gerund als Subjekt oder Objekt eines Satzes

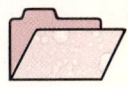

1. Complete.

a) Do you like _____ (smoke), Terry?

– No, _____ (smoke) is dangerous for my health.

b) Do you enjoy _____ (read) comics, Steven?

– Yes, I do. _____ (read) comics is great fun.

c) Do you mind _____ (get) up early, Janet? – No. I don't

mind _____ (get) up early, but not at the weekend.

d) Is _____ (play) tennis your hobby, Mike?

– Not really. I prefer _____ (cycle)

2. Translate into English. Use a gerund in each sentence.

a) Tennis spielen ist Rebeccas Lieblingssport.

_____

b) Es macht ihr nichts aus im Regen zu spielen.

_____

c) Simon liest gerne Abenteuergeschichten.

_____

d) Aber sein Hobby ist das Gitarrespielen.

_____

e) Peter kommt oft zu spät in die Schule. Er hasst es, früh aufzustehen.

_____

_____

Du wiederholst das **Gerund** als **Subjekt**, z. B. *Smoking is dangerous.* –
Rauchen ist gefährlich. bzw. als **Objekt** eines Satzes nach bestimmten
Verben, z. B. *He enjoys smoking* – Er hat Freude am Rauchen / Er hat
Freude daran zu rauchen.

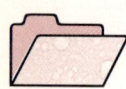

Gerund nach Präpositionen

3.   Complete: verb + preposition + gerund.

a)   Patrick apologised _____ _____ (come) late.

b)   Dawn dreams _____ _____ (travel) to California.

c)   Steven insisted _____ _____ (pay) for the ice cream.

d)   Matthew looks forward _____ _____ (work) in his holidays.

e)   James was fined _____ _____ (drive) too fast.

f)   Lindsey succeeded _____ _____ (win) the tennis match.

g)   Simon is thinking _____ _____ (go) on a cycling tour.

h)   Emma objects _____ _____ (write) the essay once again.

Du verwendest hier das Gerund nach bestimmten **Verben + Präposition**,
z. B. *apologise* + *for* + ing-Form. Lerne diese Wendungen immer mit der
dazugehörigen Präposition.

4.   Complete: adjective + preposition + gerund.

a)   Simon was proud _____ _____ (be) champion of his club.

b)   Alan is afraid _____ _____ (lose) the tennis match.

c)   Emma is fond _____ _____ (play) the piano.

d)   Darren is good _____ _____ (swim)

e)   Martin is used _____ _____ (work) hard.

f)   Rebecca is interested _____ _____ (earn) some pocket money.

g)   Most pupils are tired _____ _____ (learn) English grammar.

h)   Stuart is crazy _____ _____ (dance)

Das Gerund kann auch nach manchen **Adjektiven + Präposition** stehen, z. B. *proud + of* + ing-Form. Auch hier solltest du die Präpositionen, mit denen die Adjektive zusammengehen, kennen.

5.   Complete: noun (+ preposition) + gerund.

a)   Tom likes to sleep long; he often has trouble _____ (catch) his bus.

b)   Jane didn't feel good; she had no chance _____ (win) her tennis match.

c)   Mr Parker is a mechanic; he had no difficulty _____ (sell) his car.

d)   The bell rang; there was no time _____ (finish) the exercise.

e)   The bus arrived in time, so there was no reason _____ (be) late.

f)   What is the advantage _____ (use) this PC?

g)   I'm sorry, I had no intention _____ (push) you.

h)   Susan isn't at home, so there's no point _____ (visit) her.

Das Gerund kann nach bestimmten **Substantiven + Präposition** folgen, z. B. *chance + of* + ing-Form. Es kann auch direkt auf manche Substantive folgen, z. B. *trouble* + ing-Form.

6.   Translate into German.

a)   You can improve your English by learning more effectively.

_____

b)   You can't become a good football player without practising a lot.

_____

c)   The boys were angry after losing the game.

_____

d)   You should concentrate instead of chattering all the time.

_____

e)   They tidied their desks before leaving the room.

_____

f)   They began to laugh on hearing the news.

_____

Das Gerund folgt hier auf **allein stehende Präpositionen**, z. B. *instead of –
anstatt.* Ein wörtliches Übersetzen ist oft nicht möglich, z. B. *You can
improve ... by learning.* – Du kannst ... verbessern, indem du lernst.

Infinitiv mit *to* – Infinitiv ohne *to*

7.   Fill in the infinitive without **to** or the "to-infinitive".

a)   Paul can _____ (play) tennis quite well.

b)   He will be able _____ (join) the local team next season.

c)   The guard let Susan _____ (enter) the hall.

d)   He didn't allow all visitors _____ (enter) at one time.

e)   If you want _____ (do) the whole exercise you should

_____ (start) now.

f) We could _____ (go) to a disco if you don't want

_____ (stay) at home.

g) We ought _____ (take) a key with us, then we can

_____ (return) late.

h) Would you like _____ (have) this pen or shall I

_____ (show) you another one?

8. Translate into English.

a) Die Mädchen beschlossen, sich nächsten Samstag zu treffen.

_____

b) Helen möchte ihren deutschen Brieffreund besuchen.

_____

c) Wir mussten gestern zu Fuß nach Hause gehen.

_____

d) Wir brauchen am Samstag nicht in die Schule zu gehen.

_____

e) Peter ist krank; es wäre besser, wenn er den Arzt anruft.

_____

f) Früher lebte Ellen bei ihren Eltern; heute hat sie eine eigene Wohnung.

_____

Infinitiv ohne *to*: nach fast allen Hilfsverben (z. B. *I can go*) und *had better* (z. B. *You had better go*). **Infinitiv mit *to*:** nach *ought* (z. B. *I ought to go*) und *used to* (z. B. *He used to play*) und zahlreichen Verben (z. B. *want, decide*).

Infinitiv zur Satzverkürzung

9.   Complete. Use an infinitive after the verb and object.

a)   Karen can't sleep long. Mother wants _____

_____ (she, get up) before 7 o'clock.

b)   Jane is my best friend. She taught _____

_____ (I, use) the Internet.

c)   Helen must be punctual. We expect _____

_____ (she, be) on time.

d)   I forgot about the money. Tina reminded _____

_____ (I, give) her the £100 back.

e)   The girls were too loud. The teacher asked _____

_____ (they, be) quiet.

f)   Peter was careless. His parents would like _____

_____ (he, be) more careful in future.

g)   The boys hesitated. Their teacher encouraged

_____ (they, have) a try.

10.   Translate into English.

a)   Darren bat seine Schwester, ruhig zu sein.

_____

b)   Er erwartete, dass sie ihn nicht bei den Hausaufgaben störte.

_____

c)   Später sagte er: „Ich will, dass du mir hilfst."

_____

d)   Sie fragte: „Möchtest du, dass ich den Text abschreibe?"

_____

e)   Sie gab ihm den Rat, die Vokabeln zu wiederholen.

_____

f)   Dann fragte sie: „Willst du, dass wir den Text zusammen lesen?"

_____

Der **Infinitiv mit** *to* steht nach bestimmten **Verben + Objekt**, z. B.
want – wollen, dass; oder *would like* – möchte(n), dass. Mit dieser
Satzkonstruktion vermeidest du Nebensätze im Englischen: *I want
him to go.* – Ich will, dass er geht.

11. Rewrite the sentences using a construction with **for**.

a)   Children should not smoke. It isn't good.

   It isn't good _____

b)   You should go home now, Andrew. It's time.

   It's time _____

c)   He isn't coming. Don't wait.

   Don't wait _____

d)   This bag is too heavy for Susan. She can't carry it.

   This bag is too heavy _____

e)   Patrick learned a lot. It was important for him.

   It was _____ *a lot.*

12. Translate into German.

a)   It is important for young people to study foreign languages.

_____

b)   The weather was too bad for the plane to take off.

_____

c)   Please don't wait for me to be back for dinner.

_____

d)   There was no time for us to see the film. We had to leave.

_____

e)   Is it all right for me to stay?

_____

Der **Infinitiv mit** *to* kann nach einigen Verben / Adjektiven / Substantiven + *for* + Substantiv / Pronomen stehen, z. B. *wait for –* warten auf, *important for –* wichtig für, *time for –* Zeit für / um zu. Ein wörtliches Übersetzen ist meist nicht möglich; oft hilft ein Nebensatz mit „dass", z. B. *they were waiting for him to come –* sie warteten darauf, dass er kommt.

13. Use the infinitive.

a)   Can you tell me how I can get to the station?

Can you tell me _____ *to the station?*

b)   Peter doesn't know what he could do in such a situation.

Peter doesn't know _____ *in such a situation.*

c)   Emely wasn't sure where she could put the umbrella.

Emily wasn't sure _____ *the umbrella.*

d)   The first person who arrived was John and the last one who left was his brother.

The first person _____ *was John and the last one*

_____ *was his brother.*

e)   The most popular group that sang at the concert was XXL.

The most popular group _____ *at the*

concert was XXL. _____

14. Translate into German.

a) James didn't know which way to go. He had lost his map.

_____

b) He asked a policeman for help. This was the best thing to do.

_____

c) The policeman told him where to go.

_____

d) Helen had no idea how to prepare for the interview.

_____

e) She had also forgotten where to go.

_____

Der **Infinitiv mit _to_** kann nach **Fragewörtern** einen abhängigen Fragesatz ersetzen, z. B. (_I don't know_) _how I can get_ ▶ _... how to get_. Er steht anstelle eines Relativsatzes nach **Superlativen oder Zahlwörtern**, z. B. _the most popular group that sang_ ▶ _the most popular group to sing_.

Vermischte Übungen

15. Fill in the correct forms of the verbs in brackets.

Here is a report about some of Martin's friends.

a) Darren enjoys _____ (fly) in a plane. He likes _____ (travel) by air because it is exciting for him. He would like _____ (see) New York in his holidays.

b) Lucy, however, prefers _____ (go) by train to _____ (fly). She wants _____ (visit) Paris in August. She hopes _____ (be) able to improve her French.

c)   David doesn't like _____ (go) away at all. So he decided

_____ (stay) at home in his last holidays. This year he

is planning _____ (build) a wooden hut in the garden.

He says: "I enjoy _____ (do) practical work."

d)   Rebecca has given up _____ (smoke) She used

_____ (smoke) over twenty cigarettes a day. She says:

"I can't go on _____ (ruin) my health. I hope

_____ (be) strong enough."

e)   Simon is a computer freak. He is used _____ (sit) in

front of his computer for hours on end. He never has time

_____ (go) out, and his friends have given up

_____ (ask) him to come with them.

f)   Stuart has decided _____ (learn) Italian.

He wants _____ (visit) Rome next summer and

he is looking forward _____ (talk) to lots of Italian girls.

Überlege: Infinitiv, Gerund oder Präposition + Gerund?
Halte auseinander:
He used to go ...   Früher ging er ... und
He is used to going ... Er ist es gewöhnt, ... zu gehen

16. Ask your penfriend about his / her hobbies.

Du willst wissen, ob er / sie ...

a)   ... gern Tennis spielt;

_____

b)   ... auch nicht gern in die Disco geht;

_____

c)   ... daran interessiert ist, an einem Sommerlager teilzunehmen;

_____

d)   ... im Schwimmen gut ist;

_____

e)   ... an den Meisterschaften teilnehmen will;

_____

f)   ... sich freut dich bald zu sehen.

_____

17. Guided Writing.

You are asked to enquire about holiday apartments in Derbyshire. Use:
want, would like, look forward.

a)   Du möchtest weitere Informationen bekommen.

_I_ _____

b)   Du willst eine Ferienwohnung buchen.

_I_ _____

c)   Deine Eltern möchten den Preis für vier Personen erfahren.

_My_ _____

d)   Du freust dich auf eine baldige Antwort.

_I_ _____

18. Give your opinion.

Do you like living in your home town? Give three reasons why / why not.

_____

_____

_____

19. Translate into German.

a)   Darren can't give up smoking.

_____

b)   Julie is interested in meeting nice people.

_____

c)   Petra passed the test by studying very hard.

_____

d)   These records aren't worth buying.

_____

e)   How about having some coffee?

_____

f)   It's no use waiting any longer.

_____

g)   Grandfather used to live in an old country cottage.

_____

h)   Craig is likely to be the winner.

_____

i)   Stuart likes playing the keyboard.

_____

j)   Jonathan dislikes getting up early.

_____

Übe **freies Übersetzen**, z. B. a) ... das Rauchen aufgeben, b) ... ist daran interessiert, c) ... , indem sie tüchtig lernte, d) Es lohnt sich nicht, ... h) wird wahrscheinlich ... sein, i) ... spielt gern, j) ... steht ungern auf.

Prüfungsaufgaben

20. Give an example each for "he used to, I am used to, to use for"
and "it's no use" to show the difference in meaning. You may use
the following words: **smoke – get up early – tool – wait.**

a) _____ (1/1)

b) _____ (1/1)

c) _____ (1/1)

d) _____ (1/1)

21. Complete the following text.

Craig Kielburger from Canada is only 12, and already has got a mission.

He runs a group which is called "Free the Children". The organisation is

trying a) _____ (influence) governments

b) _____ (stop) child labour. Craig started the group after

c) _____ (read) about a 12-year-old Pakistani boy who

had been murdered because he had spoken out against exploitation of

children. Craig has already been to Geneva d) _____

(talk) to experts about the problem. These people have great difficulties

e) _____ (listen) to him because he is so young. Next

month he will fly to Asia. He wants f) _____ (support)

child workers in North Pakistan. (6)

22. Answer in complete sentences.

What are your favourite hobbies? Name two and give two reasons why you like them. You may use these words: I like …, I'm fond of …, … is my hobby. (2/4)

_____

_____

_____

23. Say whether you agree or disagree with the following statements and say why.

a) Earning money while going to school makes you independent from your parents. (2/2)

_____

_____

_____

b) Having a job and going to school don't fit together. (2/2)

_____

_____

24. Greenwich – the centre of space and time. Translate into German.

a) Two of the great puzzles throughout the centuries were how to find your way across the seas and how to tell the exact time. (3)

_____

_____

b) After working in his observatory for forty-three years the royal astronomer John Flamsteed established the Greenwich Meridian in 1676. (3)

_____

_____

c) This enabled each captain to know the exact position of his ship. (2)

_____

_____

d) In 1884 it was decided to set all clocks according to Greenwich time. (2)

_____

_____

25. Underline the four mistakes and correct them. (4)

a) Susan enjoys to play tennis in winter.

_____

b) Paul is used to get up early.

_____

c) Simon has decided to come earlier.

_____

d) Ian wants that his friends help him.

_____

e) Paul is looking forward to see Helen.

_____

I If-Sätze

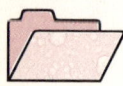 **If-Sätze vom Typ 1**

1. Complete the sentences.

a) If you do this exercise carefully, you _____
(understand) it.

b) Gary will pass his exam if he _____ (work) hard.

c) You can't succeed if you _____ (not, try).

d) What _____ (you, do) if you fail the exam?

e) If Emma comes home late, her mother _____
(be angry)

Im **if-Satz Typ 1** steht das Verb im *present* (z. B. *do, doesn't work*),
im **Hauptsatz** steht *will* (z. B. *will understand*). Anstelle von *will* kann
ein anderes **Modalverb** (z. B. *can, must*) verwendet werden.

2. Form sentences with if-clause type 1.

Emma is telling her friend Rosie about her plans for her next holidays.

a) the weather good / stay at the seaside

_____

b) go by car / certainly visit the Lake District

_____

c) find a nice place / go camping

_____

d) need a bigger tent / my friends come with me

_____

e)   there is a chance / take a boat trip on the canal

_____

f)   have a look round / pass a pretty village

_____

g)   have time / go to lovely pubs in the evenings

_____

h)   put on waterproof clothing / rain

_____

i)   take photos / send you some

_____

Vor *if* steht kein **Komma**. Beginnt der Satz mit *if*, dann setzt du ein Komma vor den Hauptsatz.

3.   **Give answers to these questions.**

a)   What will you do if you pass your exam? – **(go on holiday)**

_____

_____

b)   What will you do if you have a lot of time? – **(sleep longer in the morning)**

_____

_____

c)   What will you do if your friends give a big party? – **(try to get invited)**

_____

_____

d)   Where will you go if you visit the USA? – **(New York and the Rocky Mountains)**

_____

_____

e) When will you phone me if you are at home? – (at 7 o'clock)

_____

_____

If-Sätze vom Typ 2

4. Complete the sentences.

a) They would buy new shoes if they _____ (have)
the opportunity.

b) Gary _____ (not, ask) if he knew the answer.

c) Emma wouldn't be so good at running if she _____
(not, train) so much.

d) What _____ (can do, your friend) if he came
to visit you?

e) If you _____ (be) older, you would get a job
in your holidays.

Im **if-Satz Typ 2** steht das Verb im *past* (z. B. *had*), im **Hauptsatz** steht
would (z. B. *would buy*). Anstelle von *would* kann ein anderes **Modalverb**
(z. B. *could, might*) verwendet werden.

5. Form sentences with if-clause type 2.
Rosie is telling her friend Craig what she would like to do.

a) win a lot of money on the lottery / travel round the world

_____

_____

b) travel round the world / see a lot of interesting countries

_____

_____

c)   have a chance / first fly to New York

_____

_____

d)   be in New York / try to get tickets for the Metropolitan Opera

_____

_____

e)   go to the Metropolitan Opera / meet many nice people

_____

_____

f)   talk to many Americans / improve my knowledge of English

_____

_____

6. Answer the following questions in English.

a)   Was würdest du tun, wenn du viel Geld hättest? – (travel to New York)

If I _____

_____

b)   Was würdest du tun, wenn du in New York wärst? – (take a lot of photographs)

_____

_____

c)   Was könntest du sehen, wenn du in Manhattan wärst?
– (many skyscrapers)

_____

_____

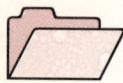

If-Sätze vom Typ 3

7.   Complete the sentences.

a)   If I had known the answer, I _____ (tell) you.

b)   What would your friend have said if you _____
(not, come) in time.

c)   If you had been ready, you _____
(can, come) with me.

d)   Tom _____ (not, be) so sad if his girlfriend
had danced with him.

e)   If Angela _____ (not, work) so hard,
she would not have succeeded.

Im **if-Satz Typ 3** steht das Verb im *past perfect* (z. B. *had known*),
im **Hauptsatz** steht *would have + past participle* (z. B. *would have told*).
Anstelle von *would* kann ein anderes **Modalverb** (z. B. *could, might*)
verwendet werden.

8.   Form sentences with if-clause type 3.

Craig is telling his friend Gary about his last holidays.

a)   save more money / spend more time in Ireland

_____

_____

b)   get better information / read books about that country

_____

_____

c)   have better information / visit more interesting places

_____

_____

d)   have the chance / take my car with me

_____

_____

e)   take my car / see more of the countryside

_____

_____

f)   the weather be not so bad / go to one of the islands

_____

_____

g)   find one of the "singing pubs" / spend an evening there

_____

_____

9.   Answer the following questions in English. Use if-clauses.

a)   Was hättest du getan, wenn du in den Ferien mehr Zeit gehabt hättest?
    – (travel to Ireland)

If I _____

_____

b)   Wo hätte Craig Rosie treffen können, wenn er in der Stadt gewesen
    wäre? – (in the cafe)

_____

_____

c)   Wohin wären sie gegangen, wenn sie sich getroffen hätten?
    – (to the cinema)

_____

_____

Vermischte Übungen

10. Complete the sentences.

Plans for a holiday

Emma: What will you do if you _____ (travel) to England
next month, Craig?

Craig: If my friend agrees, we _____ (visit) London.

I _____ (take) my camera, in case we

_____ (go) to the Tower.

Rosie: Where would you go if you _____ (have)
enough money for a long holiday, Holly?

Holly: Well, if I had enough money, I _____ (fly)
to New York. If I _____ (be) you, I certainly

_____ (stay) there for 3 months.

Joe: What would you have done if you _____ (be)
in London last winter James?

James: If I had been there, I _____ (try) to get
tickets for a musical. My friend _____ with me if

I _____ (invite) him.

in case = falls, wenn

11. Complete the following dialogue using the right tense of the verbs
in brackets.

Going to Scotland

Kirsty: If I can persuade my father, we certainly _____

(travel) to the Highlands this year.

Adam: Unless you have seen Edinburgh, you _____

(cannot say) that you know Scotland.

Kirsty: Have you made up your mind yet, whether you

_____ (come) on holiday with us?

Adam: No, not yet, because my father _____ (only give)

me the money for the journey if I _____ (pass)

my exams in May.

Kirsty: I think, you could easily succeed if you _____

(learn) a little more. If I _____ (be) you,

I _____ (pay) more attention at school.

You could be more successful at school, if you _____

_____ (not spend) all your time on the tennis court.

Adam: And I _____ (be glad) if you

_____ (not remind) me of that all the time.

unless = if not; whether = if

12. Say it in English.

Craig fragt seine Freundin Rosie,
a) was sie tun würde, wenn sie genug Geld hätte.

_____

Rosie antwortet, dass sie,
b) wenn sie so viel Geld hätte wie er, jedes Jahr zweimal Urlaub machen
würde.

_____

_____

c)   Craig sagt, dass
sie zusammen fahren können, wenn sie ihren Urlaub im Juli nimmt.

_____

_____

d)   Rosie sagt, dass sie,
wenn sie durch England reisen, ihre Freunde in Durham besuchen
werden.

_____

_____

e)   Craig sagt, dass sie,
wenn sie die Möglichkeit hätten, ihre Fahrräder mitnehmen könnten.

_____

_____

Prüfungsaufgaben

13. **If-clauses. Write down the correct form of the verbs.**

a)   (attend) If the Donaldsons didn't live on Montague Island, Michael

_____ primary school. (1)

b)   (disturb) You _____ the rare seabirds if you don't

move about quietly on the island. (1)

c)   (not be) If the island _____ a nature reserve,

many more tourists would visit it. (1)

14. **Complete the following sentences. Use the correct form
of the words in brackets.**

a)   If he had known me better, he _____

(react) differently. (1)

b)   Maybe he would be more successful if he _____

(be) older. (1)

c)   If she _____ (try) a particularly complicated

question, would the computer still understand her? (1)

d)   If an extremely fast spaceship _____ (start) out

ten thousand years ago, it _____

(cover) only six per cent of the distance of a lightyear till now. (2)

e)   But if there _____ (be) enough lifeboats on the

Titanic, many more _____

(escape) the disaster. (2)

15. Questions on the text.

a)   If you had the chance to change or stay at the same school? What would
you do? Give reason for your answer. – (stay there, don't like to leave
my friends) (1/3)

_____

_____

b)   If you were in London, what means of transport would you use?
Give one reason for your answer. – (go by bus / see more) (1/2)

_____

_____

c)   If you were offered the chance to go to school in New York for a year,
would you accept? Give three reasons for your answer.
(not / not good at English; parents not let me go / not the money /
afraid of high crime rate) (3/3/1)

_____

_____

_____

_____

_____

16. What would you do if ...?

Say **what** you would do in the situations mentioned below and say **why** you would do so. Choose **two** situations and write about **25 words** each.

a) You get the news that you have won first prize in a competition.
b) A cyclist has knocked you over as you walked home from school.
c) The police stop you on your motorbike because your passenger wasn't wearing a helmet.
d) You are at a fair and you see a child who has lost his parents.

_____

_____

_____

_____

_____

_____ (6)

17. Underline the four mistakes and correct them. (4)

a) Mr Brown would help you if you would ask him. (Herr Brown würde dir helfen, wenn du ihn fragen würdest.)

_____

b) I don't speak to you again if you don't apologize. (Ich spreche nicht wieder mit dir, wenn du dich nicht entschuldigst.)

_____

c) What would you have done if you have been in England last summer? (Was hättest du getan, wenn du letzten Sommer in England gewesen wärst?)

_____

d) If I go on holiday, I travel to Scotland. (Falls ich Ferien mache, reise ich nach Schottland.)

_____

J   Indirekte Rede

Reporting verb (= einleitendes Verb) im *present / present perfect*

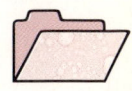

1.   Put into reported speech.

a)   Mrs Nolan says, "I want a bigger house."

_____

b)   Sam adds, "I need a room of my own."

_____

c)   The children ask, "Where are we moving to?"

_____

d)   Mr Nolan remarks, "I guess we'll have to look for a larger place."

_____

_____

e)   Mrs Nolan has always said, "We must have a house with six rooms."

_____

_____

f)   Judy says, "I'm old enough to have a room of my own."

_____

_____

g)   Mrs Nolan wants to know, "Are we going to buy a new house?"

_____

_____

Wenn das *reporting verb* im **present** oder **present perfect** steht, bleiben die Zeitformen gleich. Die **Pronomen** werden sinngemäß **verändert**. Bei der indirekten Frage übernimmst du das Fragewort der direkten Rede. **Indirekte Yes / No-Fragen** werden mit *if* oder **whether** gebildet. Beachte hier die normale **Wortstellung** (S – V – O)!

Reporting verb im *past / past perfect*

2.   **Put into reported speech.**

a)   Mr Nolan asked, "Do we want a bigger house?"

_____

b)   Mrs Nolan answered, "It is absolutely necessary for us to have six rooms."

_____

_____

c)   Sam added, "I saw an advertisement in the newspaper."

_____

d)   Judy had said, "I've always wanted a room of my own."

_____

e)   She declared, "And I like to have a room with a large window."

_____

_____

f)   Sam wanted to know, "When do we buy a new house?"

_____

g)   Mrs Nolan remarked, "I think the estate agent has got many houses for sale."

_____

_____

Steht das *reporting verb* im *past* oder *past perfect*,
verändern sich neben den **Pronomen** auch die **Zeitformen**:
*present ▶ past; past ▶ past / past perfect; present perfect ▶ past perfect;
future ▶ conditional; future perfect ▶ conditional perfect.*

Veränderungen der Modalverben

3. Put into reported speech.

a) Mr Nolan said, "We'll buy a new house if the bank gives us the money."

_____

_____

b) Judy asked, "What will we do with the old one?"

_____

c) Her father replied, "I'll go to the estate agent's and try to sell it."

_____

_____

d) Mrs Nolan remarked, "We must get a good price for the old house."

_____

_____

e) Her husband said, "You needn't worry. I can easily find a buyer."

_____

_____

f) Sam asked, "May I have a room upstairs?"

_____

g) His father answered, "You must wait until we've got an offer."

_____

_____

h) Mrs Nolan added, "If it's possible, each of us will get his own room."

_____

_____

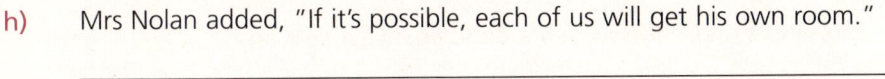

Die **Modalverben** verändern sich wie folgt: _will ▶ would;_
may ▶ might; must ▶ had to; needn't ▶ didn't have to; can ▶ could.
Could, should, would, might werden **nicht verändert**.

Weitere Veränderungen

4. Put into reported speech.

a) Mrs Nolan said, "I don't like this place any more."

_____

b) She added, "We were reading all these advertisements."

_____

c) Her husband mentioned, "I don't like it here either."

_____

d) Then he added, "I'll have a look at the newspaper today."

_____

e) Sam said, "My friend showed me his room yesterday."

_____

_____

f) Grandma declared, "I'll move out tomorrow."

_____

g) Father replied, „We'll have a larger house next week."

_____

_____

h) "Last month you just said the same", said grandmother.

_____

_____

i) Mrs Nolan said, "We missed a good chance a year ago."

_____

_____

Weitere Veränderungen bei der Umwandlung von direkter in indirekte Rede: _this ▶ that; these ▶ those; today ▶ that day; yesterday ▶ the day before; tomorrow ▶ the next / the following day; last month ▶ the previous month; a year ago ▶ a year before._

Befehl und Bitte

5. **Put into reported speech.**

a) Mrs Nolan said to Sam: "Listen to me."

_____

b) Judy said: "Please leave me alone, Sam."

_____

c) Sam shouted: "Don't lose your temper."

_____

d) Judy replied: "Don't make such a fuss about everything."

_____

e) Mrs Nolan said: "Can you speak about that problem with your father, Judy?"

_____

_____

f) Father said: "Stop quarrelling."

_____

g) Mrs Nolan said to Sam: "When you've finished, go upstairs."

_____

_____

h) She added: "Switch the lights off before you go to bed, Judy."

_____

_____

Einen **Befehl** drückst du mit _tell_ + **Objekt** + **to-Infinitiv** aus (z. B. _She told Sam_ ...). Über eine **Bitte** berichtest du mit _ask_ + **Objekt** + **to-Infinitiv** (z. B. _She asked her to_ ...).

Vermischte Übungen

6. **Put the following dialogue between Sam and Judy into reported speech.**

Judy: "Do you know that Mum is looking for a new house?"

a)   Judy asked Sam

_____

_____

Sam: "I heard her talking about this matter yesterday."

b)   _____

_____

Judy: "Do you want to move?"

c)   _____

Sam: "No, I don't want to leave here."

d)   _____

Judy: "Do you know how much a new house will cost?"

e)   _____

_____

Sam: "No, I don't; but I don't think that we can afford to buy a new one."

f)   _____

_____

Judy: "If we voted against this plan, Mum and Dad couldn't refuse our proposals."

g)   _____

_____

Sam: "What are you going to propose?"

h)   _____

Judy: "We could convert the attic into a big room."

i)   _____

Sam: "Oh! That's wonderful. I will tell Steve immediately."

j) _____

_____

7. **Mrs Nolan tells her husband what the estate agent told her on the phone.**

Agent: "My name is Bardon. I spoke to your husband about an offer last week. He asked me if I could find a suitable house for him. I've got a wonderful place which I'm sure will be large enough for your family. Can you talk about it with your family? Please let me know when you've made up your mind to move into this lovely home."

Mrs Nolan:

"Yesterday the estate agent phoned me that _____

_____

_____

_____

_____

_____

_____

_____

_____

_____

_____

_____

_____ "

Versetze dich in Mrs Nolan, die ihrem Mann erzählt, was der Makler ihr am Telefon gesagt hat. Denke an die Veränderungen, die du vornehmen musst (z. B. Zeitformen, Pronomen, Adverbien).

8.   **Put the following conversation into English. Use direct speech.**

a)   Mr Nolan sagte, dass er ein neues Haus kaufen möchte.

Mr Nolan:

"_____

_____"

b)   Die Kinder bemerkten, dass sie sehr glücklich seien, wenn jedes
ein eigenes Zimmer haben würde.

The children:

"_____

_____"

c)   Sam fragte, ob er ein Zimmer im ersten Stock haben könnte.

Sam:

"_____

_____?"

d)   Seine Mutter antwortete, dass es darauf ankomme, wie viele Zimmer
sie haben würden.

Mother:

"_____

_____"

e)   Judy fragte, wie viel ein neues Haus kosten würde.

Judy:

"_____

_____"

f)   Ihr Vater antwortete, dass sie viel Geld sparen müssten, aber er denke,
dass sie es bis nächstes Jahr geschafft haben würden.

Father:

"_____

_____

_____"

g)   Mrs Nolan fügte hinzu, dass alle helfen sollten.

Mrs Nolan:

"_____ "

Das Gespräch wird in direkter Rede wiedergegeben. Beachte dabei, dass du nicht immer wörtlich übersetzen kannst.

Prüfungsaufgaben

9.   Interpreting

You are staying at a hotel near Yosemite National Park. At the reception desk, Herr Schmid, a tourist from Germany, is trying to get some information about national parks. He does not speak English very well and asks you to do the interpreting for him.

Herr Schmid: „Ich möchte morgen den Yosemite Nationalpark besuchen und möchte gern wissen, wie ich am besten dort hinkommen kann."

You:

"_____

_____

_____ " (2)

Receptionist: "Of course, it's no problem to get there by car, but tourists usually prefer one of our bus tours."

You:

"_____

_____ " (2)

Herr Schmid: „Gut, ich fahre mit dem Bus. Darf man auch fotografieren?"

You:

"_____

_____ " (2)

Receptionist: "There will be stops at the most spectacular places of interest. Your guide will give you time enough to walk around and enjoy the scenery."

You:

"_____

_____

_____" (2)

Herr Schmid: „Vielen Dank für ihre Hilfe. Auf Wiedersehen."

You:

"_____" (2)

10. **Underline the five mistakes and correct them.** (5)

a)   Mrs Brown asked me where I am going.

_____

b)   Mr Brown asked where had his wife gone.

_____

c)   Mrs Baker says Tom to get up earlier.

_____

d)   The teacher told the boys to don't talk so loud.

_____

e)   Mr Brown wanted to know why his wife had not come earlier.

_____

f)   Mrs Brown said that she should travel to Italy next year.

_____

g)   Tom asked them where they could spend the weekend.

_____

K Partizipialsätze

Partizipien in Relativsätzen

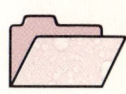

1. Replace the relative clause with the participle.

a) The train which leaves at 8 o'clock goes to Glasgow.

_____

b) The man who is knocking at the door is a milkman.

_____

c) The street which leads to the castle is very narrow.

_____

d) In our town there is a lot of pollution which is caused by too much traffic.

_____

e) Do you know the girl who is talking to Darren?

_____

f) Films which were made in Hollywood are very popular in Europe.

_____

Mit Partizipien kannst du **Relativsätze** *(relative clauses)* **verkürzen**
(z. B. *The train which leaves ...* ▶ *The train leaving ...*).

Partizipien in Nebensätzen des Grundes

2. Use particples for the clauses of reason.

a) As Darren was tired, he went to bed early.

_____, Darren went to bed early.

b) Because she felt frightened, Emma stayed at home.

_____, Emma stayed at home.

c)   As Jennifer wanted to catch the last bus, she had to leave on time.

_____ the last bus, Jennifer had to leave on time.

d)   Simon could not show his identity card as he had lost his wallet.

Simon could not show his identity card _____,

e)   As Katie didn't know the way, she had to ask a policeman.

_____, Katie had to ask a policeman.

f)   As he was injured, James could not take part in the cycling tour.

_____, James could not take part in the

cycling tour.

Mit Partizipien kannst du **Nebensätze des Grundes** *(clauses of reason)* **verkürzen**: *As* bzw. *because* = weil, da, fallen dabei weg. Beachte die veränderte Stellung des Namens im Hauptsatz: *As Darren was tired, he … ▶ … tired, Darren …*

Partizipien in Nebensätzen der Zeit

3.   Change the sentences using participles.

a)   While I was walking in the park, I met Rachel.

_____

b)   Before you hand in your report you should read it again.

_____

c)   When Lucy heard the telephone she stopped working.

_____

d)   After Andrew had helped his mother, he cycled to his friends.

_____

e)   You must be very careful when you cross the street.

_____

f)   When Mr Winter saw the taxi he stopped it at once.

_____

Mit Partizipien kannst du **Nebensätze der Zeit** _(clauses of time)_ **verkürzen**. Die Konjunktionen _while_ – während, _when_ – als und _after_ – nachdem, können weggelassen werden. Beachte die veränderte Stellung des Namens im Hauptsatz: _After Andrew had helped his mother, he cycled …_ ◗ _After … , Andrew cycled …_

Partizipien zur Verbindung von Hauptsätzen

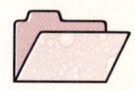

4.   Make one sentence out of two. Use a participle.

a)   Sheila walked down the lane. She sang.

_____

b)   Darren and Helen were in the kitchen. They washed the dishes.

_____

c)   Mr Miller sat in his armchair. He smoked his pipe.

_____

d)   Craig went to bed. He hoped to fall asleep immediately.

_____

e)   Karen picked up the telephone and looked forward to hearing her mother's voice.

_____

Mit Partizipien kannst du **zwei Hauptsätze zusammenfügen**. Wenn es sich in beiden Sätzen um das gleiche Subjekt handelt, kann das Personalpronomen wegfallen.

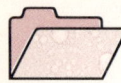

Partizip Präsens oder Partizip Perfekt?

5.   Fill in: present participle or past participle?

a)   The old lady _____ (live) next door is 92 years old.

b)   _____ (feel) he was right Peter protested against the decision.

c)   The articles _____ (sell) in the supermarket are cheap.

d)   Spanish is the language _____ (speak) in most countries
      in South America.

e)   We met a group of girls _____ (travel) to France.

f)   The number of people _____ (injure) in the accident is low.

Das **present participle** – Partizip Präsens – hat immer **aktivische
Bedeutung** (z. B. *the old lady living ...* – die alte Dame, die ... wohnt),
das *past participle* – Partizip Perfekt – immer **passivische Bedeutung**
(z. B. *The articles sold ...* – die Artikel, die ... verkauft werden).

Vermischte Übungen

6.   Write the sentences with a relative pronoun.

a)   People driving to work every day are called commuters.

      _____

b)   The girl sitting on the bench is Kathy.

      _____

c)   The car stopped by the police belongs to Fred.

      _____

d)   Trains going to Glasgow leave from platform 4.

      _____

e)   The flag flying on the roof is the Union Jack.

      _____

f)   Books bought at a flea market are cheap.

     _____

7.   **Rewrite these sentences. Begin with as / because,
       when or while.**

a)   Wanting to get home as soon as possible we hitch-hiked.

     _____

b)   Not knowing the language, Darren was helpless in France.

     _____

c)   Seeing the old man beside the road, the driver slowed down.

     _____

d)   Listening to Helen's story, the boys got very excited.

     _____

e)   Coming into the room, Jonathan heard the phone.

     _____

f)   Sitting in the pub, we could see the trains go by.

     _____

8.   **Translate into German.**

a)   Being tired, Helen sat down for a while.

     _____

b)   Peter sat on his couch reading a book.

     _____

c)   Matthew walked down the road, whistling.

     _____

d)   Being lonely herself, Jane understood Helen's problem.

     _____

e)   People wishing to visit the museum must ring the doorbell.

_____

f)   Convinced that he was right, George didn't give in.

_____

g)   Feeling very tired, Geoff went straight to bed.

_____

h)   Not wanting to lose the football match, Patrick and his friends trained
      three times last week.

_____

_____

i)   A car bought ten years ago isn't worth much today.

_____

j)   The day being fine, the children decided to play in the garden.

_____

Überlege dir die **Bedeutung** des verkürzten Satzes: Ist es ein Relativsatz
(… , der / die / das), ein Nebensatz des Grundes (… , da / weil), ein Nebensatz der Zeit (als / während) oder eine Satzverknüpfung (… und …)?

Prüfungsaufgaben

9. Complete the following text. Use the correct form of the words in brackets. (8)

Dog Steals Car

A dog a) _____ (call) Mick was arrested in the Oxford district yesterday for stealing a car. Mrs Johnson was driving from Northampton to Oxford to visit her sister, when she noticed a big, sorrowful dog at the side of the road. b) _____ (think) that the dog might have been lost she stopped the car and, c) _____ (leave) the door open, rushed to help the poor animal. As she approached, the dog suddenly leapt up and, d) _____ (rush) past her it jumped up onto the driver's seat e) _____ (put) its front paws on the steering wheel. The lady tried without success to persuade the dog to get out of the seat. f) _____ (resist) all her attempts it just sat there g) _____ (snap) whenever she got too close. Finally, h) _____ (realise) that the dog was not willing to surrender Mrs Johnson used her mobile phone to ring Oxford police station with her incredible story.

10. Make one sentence out of two and write it down. Use ing-forms.

a) Senior citizens feel stronger and more energetic these days. They don't want to give up their jobs. (1)

_____

_____

b) A lot of American teenagers work for money. They are less dependent on their parents. (1)

_____

_____

11. Translate into German.

a)   15-year-old Eni paints the soles of sports shoes, sweating in terrible heat. (3)

_____

b)   The factory employs 13,000 people wearing cheap plastic shoes because none of them can afford the shoes they make. (4)

_____

_____

c)   Eni is paid 25 cents an hour. Compared to this, a pair of tennis shoes costs about $150. (2)

_____

_____

d)   There are a lot of accidents caused by old machines. (2)

_____

_____

12. Underline the three mistakes and correct them. (3)

a)   The film which made in France is fantastic.

_____

b)   When visiting Julie, Peter wore his best suit.

_____

c)   As being cold we put on our coats.

_____

d)   There was complete silence breaking only by a train.

_____

L Wortstellung

Einfacher Aussagesatz

1. Make sentences.

a) plays / the / Ian / guitar

_____

b) Jane / her / doing / homework / is

_____

c) Russian / can / Ian / speak

_____

d) a dog / has / and / Mary / got / a cat

_____

Adverb der Häufigkeit

2. Make sentences.

a) the / swimming / boys / seldom / go

_____

b) never / drank / Susan / coffee

_____

c) together / Susan / do / and / their / Jill / homework / always

_____

d) the / Mr Miller / finish / usually / can / crossword puzzle

_____

Das **Adverb der Häufigkeit** steht vor dem Vollverb, hinter dem Hilfsverb und hinter einer Form von *to be*.

Adverbien des Ortes und der Zeit

3.   Make sentences.

a)   Mr Talbot works. – (at the weekend, often, in the garden)

_____

b)   Tom eats. – (never, in the morning, cornflakes)

_____

c)   Jean likes to listen to music. – (in her room, in the evening, usually)

_____

_____

d)   Mr Brown reads his newspaper. – (always, after breakfast, on Sunday)

_____

_____

e)   Mr Brown makes tea. – (on Sunday morning, sometimes, in the kitchen)

_____

_____

Das **Adverb des Ortes** steht meist am Satzende, das **Adverb der Zeit** meist am Anfang oder Ende des Satzes. Die genauere Zeitangabe steht vor der allgemeineren *(after breakfast on Sunday)*.

4.   Say it in English.

a)   Sage, dass dein Bruder immer mit dem Bus zur Schule fährt.

_____

_____

b)   Sage, dass du am Samstag nie Schule hast.

_____

c)   Sage, dass du manchmal am Sonntag in der Küche Tee machst.

_____

_____

d)   Sage, dass dein Freund oft am Nachmittag im Stadion Fußball spielt.

_____

_____

e)   Sage, dass ihr im Sommer selten im Fluss zum Schwimmen geht.

_____

_____

f)   Sage, dass eure Familie im Urlaub gewöhnlich zusammen Fahrrad fährt.

_____

_____

Adverb der Art und Weise – Gradadverb

5.   **Put the adverbs in the right place.**

a)   The incident happened.   **+ on a platform in London**
                                                  + last night

_____

b)   A crowd of young people were behaving …   **+ very + rudely**

_____

c)   An old lady went up to the loudest youth.   **+ slowly**

_____

d)   She found his behaviour bad.   **+ terribly**

_____

e)   The other travellers read their papers.   **+ quietly**

_____

f)   They concentrated on their papers.   + simply

_____

g)   It was surprising that they said nothing.   + really

_____

h)   The old lady's reaction was right.   + absolutely

_____

i)   The stationmaster could have told
        the youths to behave.   + more politely

_____

Das **Adverb der Art und Weise** steht meist am Satzende (nach dem Objekt, bzw. dem Verb). Das **Gradadverb** steht gewöhnlich vor dem Adjektiv bzw. dem Adverb, das es bestimmt.

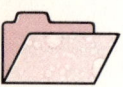

Verben mit zwei Objekten

6.   Answer the following questions.

a)   What did Tom show the controller? – (his ticket)

_____

b)   What did Jane give her mother for her birthday? – (some beautiful flowers)

_____

_____

c)   What does Mr Molyneux teach the pupils? – (French)

_____

d)   What does Mr Moneymaker promise his workers? – (higher wages)

_____

_____

e) Who did Sam send a letter to? – (Mary, not Jane)

_____

_____

f) Who does Tony lend £10 to? – (his friend, not his brother)

_____

_____

g) What will Mr Brown sell his uncle? – (his old car)

_____

h) What does Mother tell her children? – (a nice story)

_____

Nach einigen Verben können zwei Objekte stehen. Das **indirekte Objekt** steht gewöhnlich vor dem **direkten**. Willst du das indirekte Objekt betonen, dann steht es mit *to* am Satzende.

7. **Finish the sentences.**

a) Henry tried to describe _____.
   (the accident, policeman)

b) Sarah could not explain _____.
   (her father, the problem)

c) Mrs Taylor prefers _____.
   (tea, milk)

d) Mr Talbot introduced _____.
   (the landlady, himself)

e) The policeman added _____.
   (the report, another detail)

f) The pupils said _____.
   (the teacher, good morning)

Nach einigen Verben steht das **indirekte Objekt** immer mit *to* am Satzende.

Satzverbindungen mit Konjunktionen

8.   Connect the sentences with the following conjunctions:
although (2 x), **after**, **because**, **before**, **but** (2 x), **when**.

a)   Hundreds of fans had come to the airport. The plane landed.

_____

_____

b)   The fans got extremely excited. The singers came in sight.

_____

_____

c)   The singers wanted to go to their hotel. They had to sing a song first.

_____

_____

d)   The guitarist didn't want to play. He was so tired.

_____

_____

e)   Most of the fans bought tickets. They were very expensive.

_____

_____

f)   The performance had already lasted for an hour. The crowd demanded more songs.

_____

_____

g)   The crowd had asked for another song. The band began to play.

_____

_____

h)   The crowd pushed forward. The police prevented them from getting
     through.

     _____

     _____

Vermischte Übungen

9.   **Make sentences with the correct word order.**

a)   Malta / in the south of Europe / is / a small island

     _____

b)   the / and / Tower / are / in London / Buckingham Palace / sights

     _____

     _____

c)   an / in / old / England / is / Eton / public school

     _____

d)   between / autumn / winter / summer / is / the / season / and

     _____

e)   when / you / birthday / the day / were / of the year / born / your / is

     _____

     _____

f)   where / land / an airport / or / take off / a place / is / aeroplanes

     _____

g)   music / composes / a / musician / or / a / instrument / plays / musical

     _____

h)   is / a / school / live / boarding-school / pupils / where / a

     _____

10. Define the following words in complete sentences. Use the prompts.

a)   The White House – (official residence / Washington/ US president)

_____

b)   a cruise liner – (large / comfortable ship / swimming pools / hundreds of waiters / plenty of food, drinks)

_____

_____

c)   lifeboat – (on large ship / rescue passengers / ship in danger / sinking)

_____

d)   commercials – (advertisements / radio / television)

_____

e)   a holiday – (time / no school)

_____

f)   a crowd – (large number / people / together / join / place)

_____

g)   breakfast – (in the morning / first meal)

_____

h)   Denmark – (Northern Europe / small country)

_____

i)   a donkey – (animal / long ears / look / small horse)

_____

j)   a film library – (place / borrow / film)

_____

Du musst hier Definitionen von Wörtern bilden. Verwende dafür die in Klammern angegebenen Hilfen.

Prüfungsaufgaben

11. Define the following words in complete sentences.

a)   A debt: (1/2)

_____

_____

b)   An expert: (1/2)

_____

_____

c)   A dinosaur: (1/2)

_____

_____

d)   A skyscraper: (1/2)

_____

_____

e)   A burglar: (1/2)

_____

_____

f)   A housewife: (1/2)

_____

_____

g)   A computer freak: (1/2)

_____

_____

h)   A manager: (1/2)

_____

_____

12. Questions on the text. Answer in complete sentences.

The Titanic disaster was caused by a combination of bad luck, poor planning and foolish decisions. Captain James Smith's most fateful decision was to ignore the seven ice warnings he had received on Sunday, 14 April. The great ship was travelling – at nearly full speed – across the Atlantic from Southampton to New York for the first time. Then, 400 miles south of Newfoundland, a member of the crew suddenly spotted an iceberg right ahead at 11.37 p.m. A few minutes later there was a strange noise. The huge iceberg hit the Titanic, the ship, which was thought to be unsinkable. The ship was designed to be the safest with its 16 watertight compartments. Up to four compartments could be flooded without any danger to the ship.

a)   Where and when did the disaster happen? (1/1)

_____

_____

b)   What made people believe that the Titanic was unsinkable? (1/1)

_____

_____

c)   What should the captain have done to avoid the disaster? (1/1)

_____

_____

d)   How did the people on board know that the iceberg had hit the ship? (1/1)

_____

_____

Additional Question

Why do many people like to spend their holidays on ships? Give two reasons in about two sentences. (2/2+1)

_____

_____

_____

13. Letter writing

You have got a pen-friend in England and you would like to tell him / her about your holiday in Australia. Choose 5 items from the list below to write a letter of about 150 words. (20)

- natives
- food
- outback
- sports or other activities
- a picnic in a national park

- wildlife
- accommodation
- climate

- a beach party
- sights

---

*30th April,*_____

Dear _____ *,*

Guess where I am at the moment. _____

_____

_____

_____

_____

_____

_____

_____

_____

_____

Yours _____

---

14. Describe a person you know well. Refer to the points given below.

Please write about the teenager's …
- interests
- attitude towards school
- way of spending his / her time off
- relationship to parents and teachers

- opinion about politics
- view of the future

(Write about 120 words) (15)

_____
(blank writing area with lines)

15. Underline the four sentences with the wrong word order and correct them. (4)

a)   Bob met last Saturday his girl-friend Sarah at the cinema.

_____

b)   Tony reported the police the accident.

_____

c)   Sarah explained the situation to her mother.

_____

d)   Yesterday I saw on television a film.

_____

e)   The dog brings the stick his master.

_____

Lösungen

A Mengenbezeichnungen (Seite 6)

1. a) any, any, some b) any, some c) some, any d) any e) any, some f) some

2. a) Would you like some more milk? b) I'd like (to have) some more tea but without any sugar. c) Tom saw some hens on the farm, but no geese. d) Did you buy any books or CDs in town?

3. a) someone b) anywhere, anywhere c) something, anything d) something, anything, anything e) something, anything f) something, anything, something g) anyone, somewhere h) anyone i) someone

4. a) many, a lot of b) much, much c) many, many d) much, much e) many, many f) a lot of

5. a) a few b) a few c) a few d) a little e) a little

6. a) every b) Each c) each d) Every e) each f) each g) Every

7. a) Everyone in our family has got a car. b) Driving-schools can be found everywhere. c) It's impossible for a candidate to know everything. d) Today everyone must know something about cars.

8. a) anyone, anyone, someone, someone b) any, some c) anything, something d) somewhere e) everything f) everywhere

9. a) How much milk is there left? b) There is a lot of milk in the fridge, but only a little apple juice. c) There are only a few onions left. d) How many shall I buy? e) You must hurry because there isn't much time until the meal.

10. a) Michael works twenty hours in total. b) They are from India and English is their second language.

11. How much is the ticket?

12. a) How much is the new foreign language program(me)? b) Thank you very much.

13. a) Das Leben in Amerika hat sich während der letzten paar Jahrzehnte nicht verändert. b) Sie verdienen nicht genug Geld, um für jemanden zu bezahlen. c) Aber das wird nur möglich sein, wenn sie Länder wie … schlagen, von deren Spieler auch einige … spielen. d) Jedes Mal ist das Hauptereignis der Eröffnungsfeier … .

14. a) Every ◆ Each b) many ◆ much e) anyone ◆ someone

B Pronomen (Seite 13)

1. **b)** your, you **c)** He, his, him **d)** She, her, her **e)** It, its, it **f)** We, our, us **g)** You, your, you **h)** They, their, them

2. **a)** He, her **b)** They, us **c)** She, him **d)** He, him **e)** We, her **f)** He, it

3. **a)** Its **b)** His **c)** your **d)** their **e)** our **f)** her, Its **g)** your **h)** My

4. **a)** Her, She **b)** His, He **c)** They, Their **d)** Their, My, I, your

5. **a)** mine **b)** yours **c)** his **d)** hers **e)** ours **f)** yours **g)** theirs

6. **a)** his **b)** yours **c)** hers **d)** ours **e)** mine **f)** theirs **g)** His **h)** yours, mine

7. **a)** ourselves **b)** themselves **c)** itself **d)** yourself **e)** myself **f)** himself **g)** herself **h)** yourselves

8. **a)** Judy asks Tom where they can meet. **b)** Tom answers that he can't remember the cafe near the station. **c)** Judy says that a lot has changed in town last year. **d)** Tom asks if they should join the youth club. **e)** Judy says that not a lot happens there. **f)** Tom wonders if they'll meet many friends there.

9. **a)** themselves **b)** each other **c)** – **d)** each other **e)** – **f)** himself

10. **a)** We haven't seen each other for a long time. **b)** I can't help you and you must do your homework yourself. **c)** I apologise if I'm late. **d)** We enjoyed ourselves very much at the party. **e)** Tom and Mary met at the cinema.

11. **a)** who **b)** which **c)** which **d)** who **e)** who **f)** which **g)** which

12. **a)** who **b)** whose **c)** whose **d)** whose **e)** who **f)** whose **g)** whose

13. **a)** – **b)** – **c)** – **d)** which **e)** – **f)** who **g)** – **h)** who **i)** –

14. **a)** John visited the town he was brought up in. **b)** The girl you spoke to is from form 9C. **c)** This is the bus we came on. **d)** The country you are pointing to is Ireland. **e)** Is this the book you are interested in? **f)** The tourists Emma was talking to were from India. **g)** India is a country I don't know very much about. **h)** The keys you are looking for are on the shelf.

15. **a)** Simon, who is Emma's pen-friend, lives in New York. **b)** Jennifer, whose sister is in my class, will be 16 next week. **c)** Darren, who you met yesterday, joined our club. **d)** These bikes, which belong to my friends, are new.

16. **a)** – **b)** herself **c)** – **d)** themselves **e)** – **f)** – **g)** themselves **h)** herself **i)** themselves

17. **a)** The guests felt very hungry. **b)** Mr Brown mixed himself a cocktail. **c)** He couldn't remember having met so many nice people. **d)** He and his friend haven't seen each other for many years. **e)** When the bell rang, Mr Brown went to the door himself and opened it.

18.   a) whose b) who c) which d) which e) whose

19.   a) The boy, who broke his arm yesterday, must stay in hospital.
b) The young man, who rang up last night, wanted to speak to my sister.
c) A car hit a cat which was running across the road. d) In the pub there
were five men who were dirty and dangerous. e) They were waiting with
Jake whose friend was a beggar. f) The men saw two police cars which
stopped outside. g) The police interviewed a man who they thought had
stolen a car.

20.   a) The book (which, that) I read is very thrilling. b) The story (which / that)
Simon (has) told isn't true. c) The girl (who / that) Simon danced with
comes from France. d) Emma, whose sister is in Scotland at the moment,
is my friend. e) The young man, who was injured in the accident, is in
hospital.

21.   a) … is a person who runs a firm. b) … are people who come to another
country to live there. c) … is a woman who works in the home. d) …is
a huge animal which lived long ago. e) … is someone who breaks into
houses. f) … is a building which is very high. g) … is a person who is one
of the first to go to an unknown country. h) … is someone whose hobby
is working with computers.

22.   a) who, which b) which c) that (which) d) which (that)

23.   a) The athletes, who had competed in the Games, arrived in their
home town. b) Rachel whose team had won a medal was dancing around
happily. c) The winner was interviewed after the competition, which had
been really exciting.

24.   a) …is a person who protects someone or something. b) … is something
(i.e. some money) which you owe to someone. c) … is someone who
knows all about something. d) … is little pieces of paper which are
thrown about. e) … is a young person who is between 12 and 20 years.
f) … are adverts which are broadcast on TV or radio.

25.   a) Die Fabrik beschäftigt 13000 Leute, die billige Plastikschuhe tragen,
weil keiner sich die Schuhe leisten kann, die sie herstellen. b) "Für euch in
Europa sind die Schuhe, die wir herstellen, ein Sinnbild für Freiheit," sagt
sie. c) Die Fans werden die Begeisterung fühlen, die diesen Sport zum
schnellst wachsenden gemacht hat. d) Anna, die die Lehrer als äußerst
gescheit beschreiben, ist vielleicht eine Ausnahme. e) Ihr früherer
Englischlehrer sagt, dass es da Kinder gibt, die viel länger bleiben müssen.

26.   a) ~~who is standing…~~ ▸ which is standing b) ~~for it I've been waiting~~ ▸
I've been waiting for d) ~~who I was speaking~~ ▸ who I was speaking to
f) ~~we met at the party who is my girlfriend~~ ▸ who we met at the party,
is my girlfriend.

C Adjektiv – Adverb (Seite 27)

1. a) the tallest, excellent, older b) the youngest, more difficult, stronger c) the prettiest, more expensive, more, as (good) as d) more ambitious, less, fewer e) the most important, better.

2. a) happily b) quietly c) in a friendly way d) fluently e) well f) carefully g) safely h) quickly.

3. a) easy, easily, easy b) angry, angrily c) well, good d) usual, usually e) slow, slowly.

4. a) Now I can understand English well. b) My grammar isn't perfect yet. c) But I can speak fluently. d) I must still learn to spell difficult words correctly.

5. a) really boring b) terribly strict c) extremely difficult d) awfully good, really quickly.

6. a) high, highly b) near, nearly c) hard, hardly d) late, late, lately e) fair, fairly.

7. a) more carefully b) faster c) better d) more quickly e) harder f) earlier g) more seriously.

8. a) (the) fastest b) (the) most c) (the) farthest d) (the) most beautifully e) (the) most sensibly f) (the) best.

9. a) happy b) sad c) wonderful d) delicious e) good, loud f) happily g) carefully h) nice.

10. a) (Munich is) bigger than Edinburgh. b) It is the biggest city in Bavaria. c) There is one of the most important museums in Germany. d) Maybe they will build a completely new football stadium.

11. a) Ich hatte nicht die geringste Vorstellung, wie die Indianer leben, bevor ich das Reservat besuchte. b) Die Navajos sind einer der berühmtesten Indianerstämme. c) Immer mehr von ihnen wollen in Reservaten leben. d) Es ist furchtbar, wenn man hört, dass Indianer die höchste Alkoholrate im Land haben. e) Sie haben ein niedrigeres Bildungsniveau als weiße Amerikaner und schlechtere Gesundheitsbedingungen.

12. a) regularly b) popular, extremely warm c) good, really, excellent.

13. a) better, (the) quickest b) more quickly, more accurately c) worst, laziest, cleverer d) most, best, hard, effectively.

14. a) badly hurt b) particularly c) immediately

15. a) confident b) tragical c) foolish d) safest e) dangerous.

16. a) most important b) farther c) most popular d) hottest.

17. a) than b) worst c) really remarkable d) national e) more f) deep

18. huge animal. (It was) at least six metres tall and thirty metres long. (It had) thick legs like an elephant (and a) tiny head.

19. a) Als Spielberg zum ersten Mal daran dachte seinen wichtigsten Film, "Schindlers Liste", zu drehen, war er nicht sicher, ob er es schaffen / machen könnte. b) Da er glaubte, dass andere Kollegen für ein so ernstes Thema besser qualifiziert / geeignet wären, versuchte er die Rechte an erfahrenere Regisseure zu verkaufen. c) Keiner von ihnen war jedoch wirklich interessiert. d) Viele seiner Freunde sagten ihm, er würde bestimmt scheitern. e) Aber je mehr Zweifel sie äußerten, desto sicherer wurde Spielberg.

20. a) ~~beautifuller~~ ◗ more beautiful b) ~~good~~ ◗ well c) ~~well~~ ◗ good d) richtig e) ~~as~~ ◗ than f) richtig.

D   Zeitformen (Seite 38)

1. a) plays b) goes c) sits d) don't watch e) visit f) don't stay

2. a) I usually get up at seven o'clock. b) My school bus goes at twenty to eight. c) The first lesson always begins at eight o'clock. d) In the afternoon, I go to football training. e) After supper, I watch a little TV. f) On Saturday I don't get up so early as / because we don't go to school.

3. a) is tidying, is raining b) is lying (lie ◗ lying!), is reading c) are working, are repairing d) is playing, are listening e) are you doing, am repeating.

4. a) I'm just making a cake. b) Mother is celebrating her birthday. c) Susan is doing some shopping. d) She is buying coffee and flowers. e) Only Paul isn't doing anything. – Oh yes, he's playing table tennis.

5. a) decided b) didn't walk, went c) were not, was d) met, sat e) told, didn't understand, was f) entered, danced, stayed.

6. a) Last week we were in London. b) We visited Rock Circus and the Dungeon of London. c) We met some nice people and then we went to a pub. d) We had some sandwiches, but we didn't get any beer. e) The landlord wanted to see our identity cards. f) Then he said: "You're too young for alcohol."

7. a) was playing b) were swimming c) was reading d) was knitting e) was repairing f) were preparing.

8. a) was raining, went b) was writing, came, asked c) was ringing / rang, packed, ran d) was reading, came, looked e) was mending, rang.

9. a) have not seen b) has known c) have repaired d) has not tidied e) have been f) has not eaten

10. a) Julie is sad; she has lost her keys. b) We must wait; the train has not arrived yet. c) Is Patrick in? – He has just come home. d) I have tidied my room; now I can go out to play. e) I have had my bike for four years; it is still going well. f) Jenny has never been to London. What a pity!

11. a) have been working b) has been waiting c) has been raining d) have been living e) has been painting f) have been trying g) has been playing.

12. a) How long have you been learning English? – I have been learning it for five years. b) This book is not new. How long have you been using it? – We have been using it since the beginning of the school year. c) Your little brother is so dirty. – He has been playing football all morning. d) Your father is very tired. – He has been working in the garden all day.

13. a) went, had watched b) drove, had finished c) bought, had wanted d) phoned, had gone e) began, had left f) didn't come, had missed.

14. a) I am sure we will enjoy our winter holidays. b) I hope there will be enough snow. c) It will not (won't) be easy to find cheap accommodation. d) We will have to book the rooms next week. e) I will be fifteen in January. f) I think we will have a wonderful party in the snow.

15. a) Tomorrow morning there will be clouds in the mountains, b) but in the afternoon it will be sunny. c) The day after tomorrow it will be warmer, but a bit windy. d) There will be little change in the next few days. e) They are sure it won't rain.

16. a) Mr Miller is going to paint his house. b) His wife is going to buy new curtains. c) The children are going to attend a language course. d) They are not going to watch TV next Saturday. e) They are going to have a big party on Saturday night. f) They are going to have lots of food and drinks.

17. a) (They) are going to buy some CDs. b) (Helen) and her mother are going to do some shopping. Helen needs a coat. c) (Barbara) and her sister are going to buy tickets for the musical. They want to see the performance on Saturday.

18. a) met, have been going b) has had c) is working d) spends e) is saved f) will help.

19. did (you) arrive, came, was, are, had been living, lost, found, do (you) like, have not seen, have spent, do (you) like, do, are, helps, used, do (you) practise, am, have been playing, will join, Have, You're welcome.

20. a) Hello, Steven. What are you going to do in your summer holidays? b) I was in Canada last year and I liked the journey very much. I would like to go to Canada again. c) I haven't been to Canada yet. I hope I'll be able to visit my aunt in Toronto in two years.

21. a) held b) took place / had taken place c) have competed d) watch

22.   a) lives b) has just come c) is wearing d) did you buy e) were invented
       f) had experimented g) having injured / injuring h) succeeded in getting
       i) have become.

23.   a) She last saw him 88 years ago. b) He was standing on the deck of
       the Titanic. c) He hoped to see them in New York. d) They talk about it
       because it is a story of superlatives.

24.   I will get a job which (that) I really enjoy. I also hope I will find a partner
       who (that) understands my problems and that I'll get on well with my
       family.

25.   a) am writing b) have won c) would like d) is e) are f) is g) can take
       h) will come i) am looking forward j) to seeing

26.   a) Nach vier Jahren unfreiwilliger Abwesenheit wurde Vingo S. von seiner
       Frau und seinen drei Kindern spektakulär daheim begrüßt. b) Es war das
       glückliche Ende einer Geschichte, die vor vier Jahre eine tragische
       Wendung genommen hatte, als Vingo eingesperrt wurde. c) Was war das
       Verbrechen, das er begangen hatte? d) Er arbeitete in der Bank seines
       Onkels und als sein Onkel plötzlich verschwand, wurde er angeklagt, ein
       Verbrecher zu sein.

27.   a) has visited ▸ visited b) richtig c) is ▸ has been d) richtig e) has ▸ had
       f) slept ▸ was sleeping g) listens ▸ is listening.

E Fragesätze (Seite 55)

1.   a) Does school begin at eight o'clock? b) Are there lessons every
      afternoon? c) Do you have lunch at school? d) Do you go to school on
      Saturday? e) Have you visited your twin town in Germany yet?

2.   a) Are you interested in sports? b) Do you like tennis? c) Did you see the
      match last night? d) Do you want to play a game against me? e) Can you
      meet me at ten o'clock tomorrow?

3.   a) When does the first lesson begin? b) Where can the pupils buy refresh-
      ments? c) Why did Andy go to the club last week? d) How do most pupils
      work? e) How many hours does homework take a day? f) How much is
      the school uniform / How much does the school uniform cost? g) How did
      Jennifer come to school? h) When must Darren get up every morning?

4.   a) What did Simon write? b) What does Fred like? c) What did Jane buy?
      d) Who will Julia and Emma visit? e) What have they read? f) Who does
      Oliver help in the afternoon? g) What did Darren lose?

5.   a) Who loves Julia? b) Who went to Italy in her summer holidays?
      c) What happened in front of the school? d) What begins at nine o'clock?
      e) Whose friend plays the guitar? f) Which bus goes to the railway
      station? g) How many children came to the birthday party?

6. **a)** Who doesn't play cricket? **b)** Which of you doesn't know the answer?
c) Why didn't Jack stay in Dublin? **d)** When can't Sheila go home?
e) Which books don't belong to you? **f)** How many of you don't like
rugby? **g)** Who didn't come to the barbecue?

7. **a)** Where does Geoff come from? **b)** What is he good at? **c)** What / What
sort of school does he go to? **d)** Who does the old Rover belong to?
e) Who did he buy it from? **f)** What does he sometimes listen to? **g)** What
are Geoff and his friends talking about? **h)** What are they afraid of?

8. **a)** isn't she **b)** hasn't she **c)** can't she **d)** is he **e)** don't they **f)** does she
g) didn't he **h)** won't he.

9. **a)** What time do you get up every morning? **b)** How do you get to
school? **c)** Do you like school? **d)** What do you do in your spare time?
e) Which is your favourite soccer team? **f)** Do you know a German football club? **g)** Where did you learn German? **h)** Which places have you
seen so far?

10. **a)** Where do you come from? **b)** Do you have brothers or sisters?
c) How do you like Germany? **d)** What don't you like in a German school?
e) Have you been to Europe before? **f)** What are your hobbies?
g) How long are you staying / going to stay? **h)** Have you got a boyfriend?

11. **a)** Do you know any foreign languages? **b)** What schools did you go to?
c) Which were your favourite subjects at school? **d)** Which subjects didn't
you like at all? **e)** Where do you usually spend your weekends? **f)** Why
would you like to become a secretary? **g)** How are you going to come to
the office every day? **h)** When will you be able to start work?

12. **a)** How much is the ticket? **b)** Where can I buy it? **c)** When can I use it?
d) Have you ever used the Travelcard yourself?

13. **a)** When did you win your first medal? **b)** Do you know any sportsmen
who take drugs? **c)** Why did you decide to become an athlete?
d) How long do you practise every day?

14. **a)** Where are the nearest motels? **b)** How many visitors were there at the
Route 66 festival last month? **c)** Were there any serious accidents nearby?
d) Have you seen the TV series ROUTE 66?

15. **a)** Can I help you? **b)** Are there any special offers? **c)** How much is
the new foreign language programme? **d)** Can you recommend it?
e) Which exercises do customers in the U.S.A. prefer?

16. **a)** Why have you taken up a job? **b)** Are there sometimes shoplifters in
your store? **c)** What is your job like, in general?

17. **a)** ~~Who~~ ◆ Where **b)** richtig **c)** do ◆ (What) do you do **d)** richtig
e) like ◆ do you like.

F Modalverben (Seite 66)

1. **a)** can, can't **b)** will be able to **c)** wasn't able to / couldn't
   d) can, can't / aren't able to **e)** weren't able to / couldn't.

2. **a)** I'm sorry I can't help you. **b)** Yesterday I couldn't play tennis because it
   was raining. **c)** I haven't been able to phone Tom yet; I can't find his telephone number. **d)** Next Saturday I won't be able to come to training.
   e) I could help you if you rang me beforehand.

3. **a)** Can, mustn't / can't **b)** mustn't **c)** can, aren't allowed to **d)** may, can
   e) were allowed to **f)** will be allowed to **g)** haven't been allowed to.

4. **a)** During the week I am not allowed to go out / mustn't go out in the
   evening. **b)** At the weekend I can stay out / I am allowed to stay out until
   ten o'clock. **c)** Last Friday I was allowed to go to the concert. **d)** Next
   year I will be allowed to go to Italy with my girlfriends.

5. **a)** must / have to / are having to **b)** had to, Did … have to, didn't
   c) had to, didn't have to **d)** has had to **e)** will have to.

6. **a)** We must / have to learn a lot this month. **b)** Yesterday we had to write
   a long essay. **c)** Tomorrow we will have to do a difficult maths exercise.
   d) We have had to prepare a project for two weeks. **e)** On Friday, we
   need not come / don't have to come to school.

7. **a)** may **b)** may have **c)** might **d)** might have **e)** may **f)** might have.

8. **a)** should **b)** should not **c)** should **d)** should have **e)** should not have
   f) should have.

9. **a)** can, needn't, can **b)** needn't, can **c)** needn't, can **d)** mustn't
   e) Can, mustn't **f)** must, mustn't.

10. **a)** shouldn't **b)** should have **c)** needn't **d)** mustn't, should
    e) mustn't, should **f)** must, mustn't.

11. **a)** Dürfen wir hier sitzen? – Oh ja. **b)** Vielleicht regnet es morgen. Sollen
    wir unsere Pläne ändern? **c)** Könntest du mir bitte die Bushaltestelle zei-
    gen? **d)** Jennifer konnte nicht zu unserer Party kommen, weil sie letzte
    Woche krank war. **e)** Du darfst die Tür nicht offen lassen, Barbara. Es ist
    windig. **f)** Du brauchst mir nicht zu helfen, Darren. Ich kann es selber
    machen.

12. **a)** Ich kann meinen Schlüssel nicht finden. Ich muss ihn vergessen haben.
    b) Es ist schade, dass du die Vase fallen gelassen hast. Du hättest vorsich-
    tiger sein sollen. **c)** Du hättet nicht so früh kommen müssen. Das Treffen
    beginnt in einer halben Stunde. **d)** Ich winkte Peter auf der Straße zu, aber
    er reagierte nicht; vielleicht war er in Eile. **e)** Der Unfall war furchtbar. Er
    hätte noch schlimmer sein können, wenn der Krankenwagen nicht (so)
    schnell gekommen wäre. **f)** Sheila kann die Verabredung / das Datum
    nicht vergessen haben; sie ist so zuverlässig.

13. **a)** I can switch off the lights when I leave the room to save electricity. **b)** Everyone will have his spacecraft in the garage. There will be pills for all kinds of illnesses. **c)** We have to close the windows in our classroom, switch on the lights and leave the room at once.

14. **a)** should, can **b)** must not, could **c)** should.

15. **a)** Liebe Mutti, vielleicht erinnerst du dich daran, dass Jack vor drei Monaten beschloss, einen Computer zu kaufen. **b)** Seither hat es einen radikalen Wandel in seiner Haltung gegenüber seiner Familie gegeben. **c)** Jeden Tag verbringt er Stunden über Stunden an seinem Computer und probiert neue Programme aus. **d)** Sogar an den Wochenenden kann Jack nicht widerstehen, vor seinem Bildschirm zu sitzen. **e)** Ich denke, es wäre eine gute Idee, Onkel Herbert um Rat zu fragen. **f)** Er sollte in der Lage sein, mir zu sagen, was ich tun soll.

16. **a)** musst nicht ▶ darfst nicht **b)** darf ▶ vielleicht (schneit es) **c)** richtig **d)** Konntest ▶ Könntest **e)** soll ▶ sollte.

G Passiv (Seite 76)

1. **a)** is being cut **b)** are cut **c)** are repaired **d)** is being repaired **e)** is being tested **f)** are not tested

2. **a)** was being cleaned **b)** was cleaned **c)** was being built **d)** were built **e)** are served **f)** were being served

3. **a)** have been stolen **b)** has been written **c)** have been given **d)** have been solved **e)** has been done **f)** has not been allowed **g)** has not been found **h)** has never been invited

4. **a)** won't / will not be repaired **b)** will be shown **c)** will be asked **d)** will be smashed **e)** will be opened **f)** will be invited **g)** will not / won't be completed **h)** will be developed

5. **a)** should be washed **b)** cannot be shut **c)** ought to be tidied **d)** could not be seen **e)** must be looked after **f)** might be invited **g)** has to be pulled down **h)** cannot be learned **i)** ought not to be laughed at **j)** can only be done **k)** must be sold **l)** has to be done **m)** must not be entered **n)** could not be put out

6. **a)** is understood **b)** will be invited **c)** was shown **d)** is earned **e)** will be won **f)** was built **g)** has not been finished **h)** will be finished **i)** must be discussed **j)** is not taught **k)** has always been **l)** has been made **m)** is being repaired **n)** was being built

7. **a)** took place **b)** were celebrated **c)** took place **d)** were, were held **e)** included **f)** were treated **g)** renewed **h)** have been held **i)** applies, must be built **j)** have been invited **k)** are shown

8. **a)** Man bot Frau Carter eine bessere Arbeit an. **b)** Gestern Abend wurde der Doktor geholt. **c)** Man wird der Mannschaft eine große Möglichkeit bieten. **d)** Mr Johnson soll (angeblich) nächste Woche nach Paris fliegen. **e)** Man sagte, dass Herr Brown einen anderen Job finden würde.

9. **a)** A ferry to England must be booked very early. **b)** A letter was written to me. **c)** I was offered a good hotel. **d)** I will be sent a good offer soon. **e)** My friend has also been invited.

10. **a)** was fascinated **b)** was asked **c)** were damaged (had been damaged) **d)** was interviewed **e)** were taken **f)** was chosen (had been chosen)

11. **a)** Man wird dir wahrscheinlich später glauben. **b)** Ich habe einen Film gemacht, der der teuerste genannt worden ist. **c)** Die meisten Stuntleute wurden ernstlich verletzt. **d)** Seit damals werden die Olympischen Spiele wieder abgehalten. **e)** Man bezahlt Eni 25 Cents die Stunde. **f)** Sie werden oft gezwungen, bis Mitternacht zu arbeiten. (Sie müssen…) **g)** Zwei Finger sind abgetrennt worden.

12. **a)** ~~is worn~~ ▸ are worn **b)** ~~is being frying~~ ▸ is being fried **d)** ~~are drove~~ ▸ are driven **e)** ~~must be keeping~~ ▸ must be kept **f)** Tony sagte, er sei ein guter Spieler. ▸ Man sagt, Tony sei ein guter Spieler. (Tony soll ein guter Spieler sein.)

H   Gerund – Infinitiv (Seite 85)

1. **a)** smoking, smoking **b)** reading, reading **c)** getting, getting **d)** playing, cycling.

2. **a)** Playing tennis is Rebecca's favourite sport. **b)** She doesn't mind playing in the rain. **c)** Simon likes reading adventure stories. **d)** But his hobby is playing the guitar. **e)** Peter often comes to school late. He hates getting up early.

3. **a)** for coming **b)** of travelling **c)** on paying **d)** to working **e)** for driving **f)** in winning **g)** of going **h)** to writing.

4. **a)** of being **b)** of losing **c)** of playing **d)** at swimming **e)** to working **f)** in earning **g)** of learning **h)** about dancing.

5. **a)** catching **b)** of winning **c)** (in) selling **d)** for finishing **e)** for being **f)** of using **g)** of pushing **h)** in visiting.

6. **a)** Du kannst dein Englisch verbessern, indem du effektiver lernst. **b)** Du kannst kein guter Fußballer werden, ohne viel zu trainieren. **c)** Die Buben waren verärgert, nachdem sie das Spiel verloren hatten. **d)** Du solltest dich konzentrieren, anstatt die ganze Zeit zu schwätzen. **e)** Sie reinigten ihre Tische, bevor sie das Zimmer verließen. **f)** Sie fingen an zu lachen, als sie die Neuigkeit hörten.

7. a) play b) to join c) enter d) to enter e) to do, start f) go, to stay
    g) to take, return h) to have, show.

8. a) The girls decided to meet next Saturday. b) Helen would like to visit
    her German pen-friend. c) We had to walk home yesterday. d) We needn't
    go to school on Saturday. e) Peter is ill; he had better call his doctor.
    f) Ellen used to live with her parents; today she has a flat of her own.

9. a) her to get up b) me to use c) her to be d) me to give e) them to be
    f) him to be g) them to have.

10. a) Darren asked his sister to be quiet. b) He expected her not to disturb
    him with his homework. c) Later he said: "I want you to help me".
    d) She asked: "Would you like me to copy the text?" e) She advised him
    to repeat the vocabulary. f) Then she asked: "Do you want us to read the
    text together?"

11. a) for children / them to smoke b) for you to go home c) for him to come
    d) for Susan / her to carry e) important for Patrick / him to learn.

12. a) Es ist wichtig für junge Menschen, Fremdsprachen zu lernen. b) Das
    Wetter war zu schlecht, als dass das Flugzeug abheben / starten konnte.
    c) Warte(t) bitte nicht darauf, dass ich zum Essen zurück bin. d) Es war
    keine Zeit, dass wir uns den Film ansahen. Wir mussten fort. e) Geht es
    in Ordnung, wenn ich bleibe?

13. a) how to get b) what to do c) where to put d) to arrive, to leave
    e) to sing.

14. a) James wusste nicht, welchen Weg er einschlagen sollte. Er hatte seine
    Landkarte verloren. b) Er bat einen Polizisten um Hilfe. Das war das Beste,
    was er tun konnte. c) Der Polizist sagte ihm, wo er gehen sollte. d) Helen
    hatte keine Idee, wie sie sich auf das Interview / Vorstellungsgespräch
    vorbereiten sollte. e) Sie hatte auch vergessen, wo sie hingehen sollte.

15. a) flying, travelling, to see b) going, flying, to visit, to be c) going, to stay,
    to build, doing d) smoking, to smoke, ruining, to be / I'll be e) to sitting,
    for going, asking f) to learn, to visit, to talking.

16. a) Do you like playing tennis / Are you fond of playing tennis? b) Do you
    also dislike / hate going to the disco? c) Are you interested in taking part
    in a summer camp? d) Are you good at swimming? e) Do you want to
    participate in the championships? f) Are you looking forward to seeing
    me soon?

17. a) (I) would like to obtain / get further information. b) (I) want to book a
    holiday apartment. c) (My) parents would like to find out the price for four
    persons. d) (I) look forward to receiving / getting an answer soon.

18. My home town is (not) situated in a very beautiful area. There is (not) a lot
    to do. The people are (not) very friendly.

19. **a)** Darren kann das Rauchen nicht aufgeben. **b)** Julie ist daran interessiert, nette Leute zu treffen. **c)** Petra bestand die Prüfung, indem sie tüchtig lernte. **d)** Es lohnt sich nicht, diese Platten zu kaufen. **e)** Wie wär's mit etwas Kaffee / , wenn wir Kaffee trinken? **f)** Es hat keinen Zweck, länger zu warten. **g)** Großvater hat früher in einem alten Landhaus gewohnt. **h)** Craig wird wahrscheinlich gewinnen / der Sieger sein. **i)** Stuart spielt gern Keyboard. **j)** Jonathan steht ungern / nicht gern früh auf.

20. **a)** My father used to smoke as a young man. **b)** I am used to getting up early. **c)** You can use this tool for cutting. d) It's no use waiting for Susan any longer.

21. **a)** to influence **b)** to stop **c)** reading / he had read **d)** to talk **e)** listening / in listening **f)** to support

22. My favourite hobbies are soccer and tennis. I'm fond of soccer because I like playing in a team. Playing tennis is good exercise for me, and I can meet lots of people in our local club.

23. **a)** I agree because you can buy things that are your taste, or you can travel where you like without your parents. / I disagree because my parents are willing to give me enough pocket money and I want to concentrate on my school work. **b)** I agree because you have to work hard at school to get reasonable marks. / I can't agree because this is a question of organising ability to do well in both.

24. **a)** Zwei der großen Rätsel über die Jahrhunderte waren, wie man den Weg über die Meere findet und wie man die genaue Uhrzeit bestimmen kann. **b)** Nachdem er 43 Jahre in seinem Observatorium gearbeitet hatte, legte der königliche Astronom John Flamsteed 1676 den Meridian von Greenwich fest. **c)** Dies versetzte jeden Kapitän in die Lage, die genaue Position seines Schiffes zu kennen. **d)** 1884 wurde beschlossen, alle Uhren nach der Zeit von Greenwich zu stellen.

25. **a)** to play ▸ playing **b)** to get ▸ to getting **c)** richtig **d)** that his friends help ▸ his friends to help **e)** to see ▸ to seeing.

I   If-Sätze (Seite 100)

1. **a)** will understand **b)** works **c)** don't try **d)** will you do **e)** will be angry

2. **a)** If the weather is good, I'll stay at the seaside. **b)** If we go by car, we'll certainly visit the Lake District. **c)** If we find a nice place, we'll go camping. **d)** We will need a bigger tent if my friends come with me. **e)** If there is a chance, we'll take a boat trip on the canal. **f)** We'll have a look around if we pass a pretty village. **g)** If we have time, we'll go to lovely pubs in the evenings. **h)** We'll put on waterproof clothing if it rains. **i)** If I take photos, I'll send you some.

3. **a)** If I pass my exam, I'll go on holiday. **b)** If I have a lot of time, I'll sleep longer in the morning. **c)** If my friends give a big party, I'll try to get invited. **d)** If I visit the USA, I'll go to New York and the Rocky Mountains. **e)** If I'm at home, I'll phone you at 7 o'clock.

4. **a)** had **b)** would not ask **c)** didn't train **e)** could your friend do **f)** were

5. **a)** If I won a lot of money on the lottery, I would travel round the world. **b)** If I travelled round the world, I would see a lot of interesting countries. **c)** If I had a chance, I would first fly to New York. **d)** If I were (was) in New York, I would try to get tickets for the Metropolitan Opera. **e)** If I went to the Metropolitan Opera, I would meet many nice people. **f)** If I talked to many Americans, I would improve my knowledge of English.

6. **a)** If I had a lot of money, I would travel to New York. **b)** If I was in New York, I would take a lot of photographs. **c)** If I was in Manhattan, I could see many skyscrapers.

7. **a)** would have told **b)** had not come **c)** could have come **d)** would not have been **e)** had not worked

8. **a)** If I had saved more money, I would have spent more time in Ireland. **b)** I would have got better information if I had read books about that country. **c)** If I had had better information, I would have visited more interesting places. **d)** If I had had the chance, I would have taken my car with me. **e)** If I had taken my car with me, I would have seen more of the countryside. **f)** If the weather hadn't been so bad, I would have gone to one of the islands. **g)** If I had found one of the "singing pubs", I would have spent an evening there.

9. **a)** If I had had more time in my holidays, I would have travelled to Ireland. **b)** Craig could have met Rosie in the cafe if he had been in town. **c)** If they had met, they would have gone to the cinema.

10. travel; will visit, will take, go; had; would fly, was (were), would stay; had been; would have tried, would have gone, had invited

11. will travel; cannot say; will come; will only give, pass; learnt, was (were), would pay, did not spend; would be glad, didn't remind

12. **a)** What would you do Rosie if you had enough money? **b)** If I had as much money as you, I would go on holiday twice a year. **c)** We can travel together if you take your holiday in July. **d)** If we travel through England, we will visit our friends in Durham. **e)** If we had the chance, we could take our bikes with us.

13. **a)** would attend **b)** will disturb **c)** wasn't

14. **a)** would have reacted **b)** was (were) **c)** tried **d)** had started, would have covered **e)** had been, would have escaped

15. a) I would stay there because I wouldn't like to leave my friends.
     b) If I were in London, I would go by bus because I could see more of the
     town. c) I don't think I would go because I'm not good at English. My
     parents would not let me go because they don't have the money and they
     are afraid of the high crime rate.

16. a) If I won first prize in a competition, I would definitely go on holiday but
     I would also save some of the money. b) If a cyclist knocked me over, I
     would probably shout at him and then I would try to walk home. c) If the
     police stopped me, I would tell them that my friend had been wearing a
     helmet when we left but it had fallen off. We were driving back to find it.
     d) If I saw a lost child at a fair, I would try to make sure he (she) was safe
     by taking him (her) to a policeman.

17. a) would ask ▶ asked b) don't speak ▶ won't speak
     c) have been ▶ had been d) travel ▶ will travel

J   Indirekte Rede (Seite 111)

1.   a) Mrs Nolan says (that) she wants a bigger house. b) Sam adds (that) he
     needs a room of his own. c) The children ask where they are moving to.
     d) Mr Nolan remarks (that) he guesses they will have to look for a larger
     place. e) Mrs Nolan has always said (that) they must have a house with six
     rooms. f) Judy says (that) she is old enough to have a room of her own.
     g) Mrs Nolan wants to know if they are going to buy a new house.

2.   a) Mr Nolan asked if they wanted a bigger house. b) Mrs Nolan answered
     (that) it was absolutely necessary for them to have six rooms.
     c) Sam added (that) he saw (had seen) an advertisement in the newspaper.
     d) Judy had said (that) she had always wanted a room of her own.
     e) She declared (that) she liked to have a room with a large window.
     f) Sam wanted to know when they bought a new house. g) Mrs Nolan
     remarked (that) she thought the estate agent had got many houses for
     sale.

3.   a) Mr Nolan said (that) they would buy a new house if the bank gave
     them the money. b) Judy asked what they would do with the old one.
     c) Her father replied (that) he would go to the estate agent's and try to sell
     it. d) Mrs Nolan remarked (that) they had to get a good price for the old
     house. e) Her husband said (that) she didn't have to worry and he could
     easily find a buyer. f) Sam asked if he might have a room upstairs.
     g) His father answered that he had to wait until they had got an offer.
     h) Mrs Nolan added that if it was possible, each of them would get his
     own room.

4. **a)** Mrs Nolan said she didn't like that place any more. **b)** She added they were (had been) reading all those advertisements. **c)** Her husband mentioned he didn't like it there either. **d)** Then he added he would have a look at the newspaper that day. **e)** Sam said his friends showed (had shown) him his room the day before. **f)** Grandma declared she would move out the following day. **g)** Father replied they would have a larger house the following week. **h)** Grandmother said he just said (had said) the same the previous month. **i)** Mrs Nolan said they missed (had missed) a good chance the year before.

5. **a)** Mrs Nolan told Sam to listen to her. **b)** Judy asked Sam to leave her alone. **c)** Sam told her not to lose her temper. **d)** Judy told him not to make such a fuss about everything. **e)** Mrs Nolan asked Judy to speak about that problem with her father. **f)** Father told them to stop quarrelling. **g)** Mrs Nolan told Sam to go upstairs when he had finished. **h)** She told Judy to switch off the lights before she went to bed.

6. **a)** … if he knew that Mum was looking for a new house. **b)** Sam answered (that) he (had) heard her talking about that matter the day before. **c)** Judy asked if Sam wanted to move. **d)** Sam answered (that) he didn't want to leave there. **e)** Judy wanted to know if he knew how much a new house would cost. **f)** Sam answered that he didn't, but he didn't think they could afford to buy a new one. **g)** Judy said that if they voted against that plan, Mum and Dad couldn't refuse their proposals. **h)** Sam asked what she was going to propose. **i)** Judy replied (that) they could convert the attic into a big room. **j)** Sam exclaimed (that) that was wonderful and he would tell Steve immediately.

7. … he had spoken to you about an offer the week before. He said you had asked him if he could find a suitable house for you. He added (that) he had got a wonderful place which he was sure would be large enough for our family. Then he asked if I could talk about it with my family. Then he asked me to let him know when we had made up our mind to move into that lovely home.

8. **a)** I'd like to buy a new house. **b)** We would be very happy if we had our own room. **c)** Could I have a room on the first floor (upstairs)? **d)** It depends on how many rooms we will have. **e)** How much will a new house cost? **f)** We'll have to save a lot of money, but I think we'll have managed it by next year. **g)** Everyone of us should help.

9. Mr Schmid would like to visit Yosemite National Park tomorrow and he would like to know the best way to get there. – Es ist natürlich kein Problem, mit dem Auto dorthin zu gelangen, aber die Touristen bevorzugen gewöhnlich einen unserer Busausflüge. – Okay then, he will go by bus. Is he allowed to take photos? – An den interessantesten Plätzen gibt es einen Aufenthalt. Ihr Reiseleiter wird ihnen genug Zeit geben, herumzuspazieren und die Landschaft zu genießen. – Mr Schmid thanks a lot for your help and says good-bye.

10.   a) I am going ◆ I was going b) where had his wife gone ◆ where his wife had gone c) Mrs Baker ~~says~~ Tom ◆ Mrs Baker tells Tom d) told the boys ~~to don't~~ talk so loud ◆ told the boys not to talk so loud. f) next year ◆ the following year.

K   Partizipialsätze (Seite 121)

1.   a) The train leaving … b) The man knocking … c) The street leading … d) In our town there is a lot of pollution caused … e) Do you know the girl talking … f) Films made in Hollywood …

2.   a) Being tired b) Feeling frightened c) Wanting to catch d) having lost his wallet e) Not knowing the way f) Being injured.

3.   a) While walking … b) Before handing in … c) (On) hearing the telephone Lucy stopped working … d) After having helped / After helping / Having helped his mother, Andrew cycled … e) (when) crossing … f) Seeing the taxi Mr Winter stopped …

4.   a) Sheila walked down the lane singing. b) Darren and Helen were in the kitchen washing the dishes. c) Mr Miller sat in his armchair smoking his pipe. d) Craig went to bed hoping to fall asleep immediately. e) Karen picked up the telephone looking forward to hearing her mother's voice.

5.   a) living b) Feeling c) sold d) spoken e) travelling f) injured.

6.   a) People who drive to work … b) The girl who is sitting … c) The car which was stopped … d) Trains which go to Glasgow … e) The flag which is flying … f) Books which are bought …

7.   a) As / Because we wanted to get home … b) As / Because he didn't know … c) When he saw the old man … d) While they were listening to Helen's story … e) When he came into the room … f) While we were sitting in the pub …

8.   a) Da / Weil sie müde war, setzte sich Helen eine Zeitlang hin. b) Peter saß auf seiner Couch und las ein Buch. c) Matthew ging die Straße entlang und pfiff. d) Da / weil sie selber einsam war, verstand Jane Helens Problem. e) Leute, die das Museum besuchen wollen, müssen die Türglocke läuten. f) Da / Weil er überzeugt war, Recht zu haben, gab George nicht nach. g) Da / weil er sich sehr müde fühlte, ging Geoff sofort ins Bett. h) Da / Weil sie das Fußballspiel nicht verlieren wollten, trainierten Patrick und seine Freunde letzte Woche dreimal. i) Ein Auto, das vor zehn Jahren gekauft wurde, ist heute nicht viel wert. j) Da / Weil der Tag schön war, beschlossen die Kinder im Garten zu spielen.

9.   a) called b) Thinking c) leaving d) rushing e) putting f) Resisting g) snapping h) realising.

10.   a) Feeling stronger and more energetic these days senior citizens don't want to give up their jobs. b) (As they are) Working for money a lot of American teenagers are less dependent on their parents.

11.   a) Die 15-jährige Eni bemalt die Sohlen von Sportschuhen, wobei sie in der schrecklichen Hitze schwitzt. b) Die Fabrik beschäftigt 13.000 Menschen, die Plastikschuhe tragen, weil sich keiner von ihnen die Schuhe, die sie herstellen, leisten kann. c) Man bezahlt Eni 25 Cents pro Stunde. Im Vergleich dazu / Verglichen damit kostet ein Paar Tennisschuhe ungefähr 150 Dollar. d) Es gibt viele Unfälle, die durch alte Maschinen verursacht werden.

12.   a) which ◆ (the film) made / the film which was made b) richtig c) As ◆ Being cold d) breaking ◆ broken.

L   Wortstellung (Seite 129)

1.   a) Ian plays the guitar. b) Jane is doing her homework. c) Ian can speak Russian. d) Mary has got a dog and a cat.

2.   a) The boys seldom go swimming. b) Susan never drank coffee. c) Susan and Jill always do their homework together. d) Mr Miller can usually finish the crossword puzzle.

3.   a) Mr Talbot often works in the garden at the weekend. b) Tom never eats cornflakes in the morning. c) Jean usually likes to listen to music in her room in the evening. d) Mr Brown always reads his newspaper after breakfast on Sunday. e) Mr Brown sometimes makes tea in the kitchen on Sunday morning.

4.   a) My brother always goes to school by bus. b) I never have school on Saturday. c) I sometimes make tea in the kitchen on Sunday. d) My friend often plays football in the stadium in the afternoon. e) We seldom go swimming in the river in summer. f) Our family usually goes cycling together in our holidays.

5.   a) The incident happened on a platform in London last night. b) A crowd of young people were behaving very rudely. c) An old lady slowly went up to the loudest youth. d) She found his behaviour terribly bad. e) The other travellers quietly read their papers. f) They simply concentrated on their papers. g) It was really surprising that they said nothing. h) The old lady's reaction was absolutely right. i) The stationmaster could have told the youths to behave more politely.

6.   a) Tom showed the controller his ticket. b) Jane gave her mother some beautiful flowers for her birthday. c) Mr Molyneux teaches the pupils French. d) Mr Moneymaker promises his workers higher wages. e) Sam sent a letter to Mary, not to Jane. f) Tony lends £10 to his friend,

not to his brother. **g)** Mr Brown will sell his uncle his old car. **h)** Mother tells her children a nice story.

7. **a)** … the accident to the policeman. **b)** … the problem to her father. **c)** … tea to milk. **d)** … himself to the landlady. **e)** … another detail to the report. **f)** … good morning to the teacher.

8. **a)** Hundreds of fans had come to the airport before the plane landed. **b)** The fans got extremely excited when the singers came in sight. **c)** The singers wanted to go to their hotel but they had to sing a song first. **d)** The guitarist didn't want to play because he was so tired. **e)** Most of the fans bought tickets although they were very expensive. **f)** The performance had already lasted for an hour but the crowd demanded more songs. **g)** After the crowd had asked for another song, the band began to play. **h)** The crowd pushed forward although the police prevented them from getting through.

9. **a)** Malta is a small island in the south of Europe. **b)** The Tower and Buckingham Palace are sights in London. **c)** Eton is an old public school in England. **d)** Autumn is the season between summer and winter. **e)** Your birthday is the day of the year when you were born. **f)** An airport is a place where aeroplanes land or take off. **g)** A musician composes music or plays a musical instrument. **h)** A boarding-school is a school where pupils live.

10. **a)** The White House is the official residence of the US president in Washington. **b)** A cruise liner is a large and comfortable ship with swimming pools and hundreds of waiters. You get plenty of food and drink there. **c)** Lifeboats must be on large ships to rescue passengers when the ship is in danger of sinking. **d)** Commercials are advertisements on radio and television. **e)** A holiday is the time when we have no school. **f)** A crowd is a large number of people joined together in a place. **g)** Breakfast is the first meal in the morning. **h)** Denmark is a small country in Northern Europe. **i)** A donkey is an animal with long ears which looks like a small horse. **j)** A film library is a place where you can borrow films.

11. **a)** … is a sum of money you owe someone / which you have to pay back. **b)** … is someone who knows a lot in a special field. **c)** … was a prehistoric animal. **d)** … is a very high building. In Manhattan, there are a lot of skyscrapers. **e)** … breaks into houses and steals things. **f)** … is a woman who does the cooking, cleaning and shopping for her family. **g)** … is a person who is very interested in computers. **h)** … is a person who is responsible for running a firm.

12. **a)** The disaster happened 400 miles south of Newfoundland at 11.37 p.m. **b)** They believed that the Titanic was unsinkable because of the 16 watertight compartments. **c)** The captain should not have ignored the seven warnings. **d)** There was a strange noise.

Additional Question

I think they want to have a luxury holiday. They can visit different places and needn't drive their own car. (+1) They can leave one place in the evening and be somewhere else in the morning.

13.　　… You won't believe it, but I'm in Australia. We arrived in Sydney five weeks ago. It seemed awfully hot there since we had left Frankfurt in cold and rainy weather. Then we went to the outback to visit Australia's sight Ayers Rock. It was spectacular. The climate was dry and even hotter than in Sydney. Our accommodation was quite simple. We lived in tents and cooked our meals together. The food was okay although we very often had to live on tinned food. You can't find many supermarkets in Australia's outback. Anyway, we had a wonderful time and met many interesting people. I was very fascinated to learn about Australia's native people who are called Aborigines. There are special programmes to teach Aboriginal children about their own culture. A great idea, isn't it? How about your holiday?

14.　　He likes doing sports especially team games like handball. But he is also interested in computer games and internet surfing. Apart from this, he likes to meet his friends at weekends. He enjoys school though not every subject. It depends on the teacher. Above all he prefers sciences but does fairly well in languages, too. He likes his parents but he doesn't spend much time with them. They have to work long hours and at the weekends, he is often not at home. As far as his teachers are concerned, it is very different. Some are really boring others give interesting lessons you can profit from even outside school. He quite often goes to handball matches with his friends. As he is a computer fan, he also likes to talk a lot about bytes and bits. Once a week he practises with his handball team. He is not very interested in politics but he is, however, informed about current events and political parties. He is not really pessimistic about the future although he recognises the threat of unemployment. Nobody knows how things will develop, so it is no use being too frightened.

15.　　a) last Saturday ▸ Last Saturday Bob met his girlfriend Sarah at the cinema.
　　　b) … the police the accident ▸ Tony reported the accident to the police.
　　　d) … on television a film ▸ Yesterday I saw a film on television.
　　　e) … the stick his master ▸ The dog brings his master the stick.